# ESSENTIAL *Vaishnava* TEACHINGS

# ESSENTIAL *Vaishnava* TEACHINGS

## THE PATH *of* PURE DEVOTION

*Timeless Questions ✥ Timeless Answers*

Swami B.B. Bodhayan

MANDALA
PUBLISHING
PO Box 3088
San Rafael, CA 94912
www.mandalaearth.com
info@mandala.org

Find us on Facebook: www.facebook.com/mandalaearth
Follow us on Twitter: @mandalaearth



Published by Mandala Publishing, San Rafael, California, in 2019.


Library of Congress Cataloging-in-Publication Data available.

ISBN: 978-1-68383-851-7

Readers interested in the subject matter should visit the Gopinath Gaudiya Math website at www.gopinathgaudiyamath.com or write to:

Ishodyan, Sri Mayapur
District Nadia, West Bengal
India, 741313

Manufactured in India
10 9 8 7 6 5 4 3 2

*vande 'haṁ śrī-guroḥ śrī-yuta-pada-kamalaṁ śrī-gurūn vaiṣṇavāṁś ca*
*śrī-rūpaṁ sāgrajātaṁ saha-gaṇa-raghunāthānvitaṁ taṁ sa-jīvam*
*sādvaitaṁ sāvadhūtaṁ parijana-sahitaṁ kṛṣṇa-caitanya-devaṁ*
*śrī-rādhā-kṛṣṇa-pādān saha-gaṇa-lalitā-śrī-viśākhānvitāṁś ca*

I offer my most respectful obeisances unto the lotus feet of my divine preceptor and my instructing gurus. I offer my most respectful obeisances unto all the Vaiṣṇavas and unto the Six Gosvāmīs, including Śrīla Rūpa Gosvāmī, Śrīla Sanātana Gosvāmī, Raghunātha Dāsa Gosvāmī, Jīva Gosvāmī, and their associates. I offer my respectful obeisances unto Śrī Advaita Ācārya Prabhu, Śrī Nityānanda Prabhu, Śrī Caitanya Mahāprabhu, and all His devotees, headed by Śrīvāsa Ṭhākura. I then offer my respectful obeisances unto the lotus feet of Lord Kṛṣṇa, Śrīmatī Rādhārāṇī, and all the *gopīs*, headed by Lalitā and Viśākhā.

Śrīla Bhakti Pramode Purī Gosvāmī Ṭhākura
Founder Ācārya, Śrī Gopīnātha Gauḍīya Maṭha

Śrīla Bhaktisiddhānta Sarasvatī Ṭhākura Prabhupāda

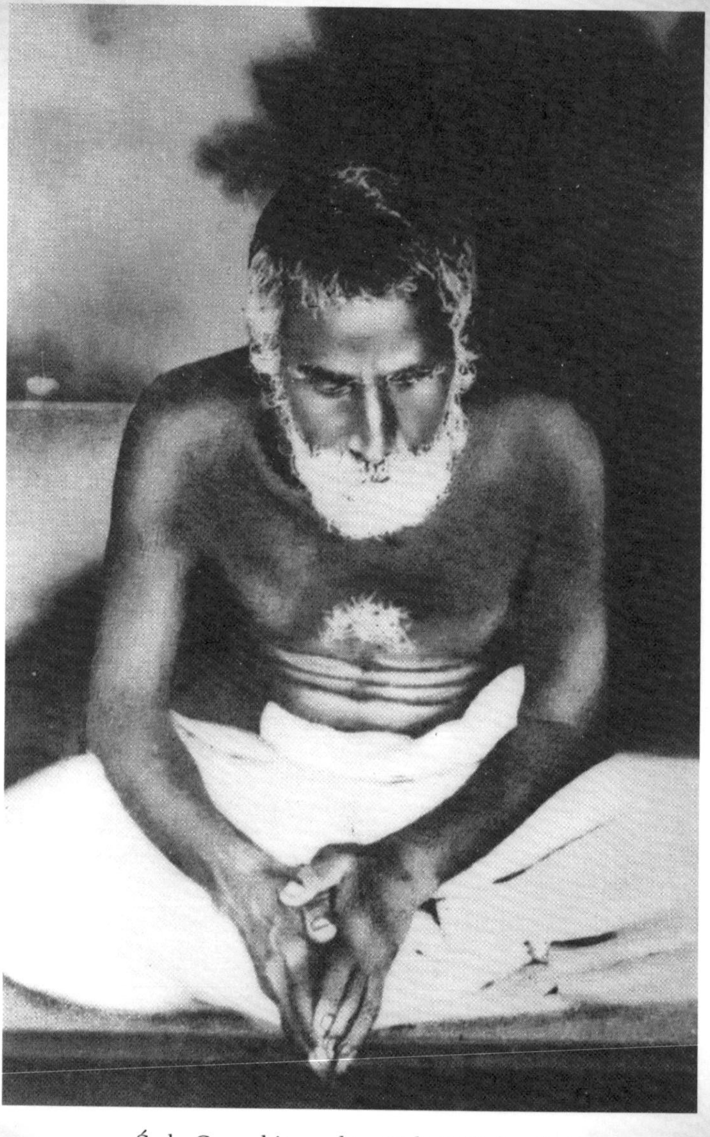

Śrīla Gaurakiśora dāsa Bābājī Mahārāja

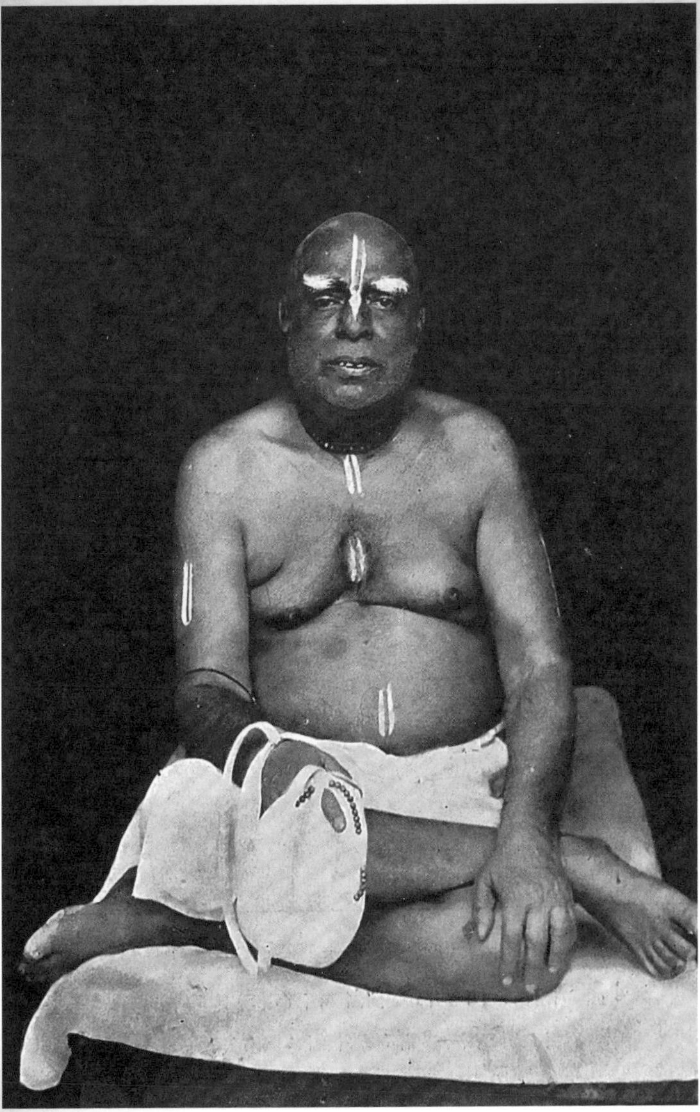

Śrīla Saccidānanda Bhaktivinoda Ṭhākura

# Contents

Preface
13

I: The Soul and God
15

II: Guru Parampara
37

III: Vaishnava Dharma
and Sadhana
105

Pronunciation Guide
178

Short Biographies of
Our Lineage
181

About the Author
188

Śrīla Bhakti Bibudha Bodhāyan Mahārāja
President Ācārya, Śrī Gopīnātha Gauḍīya Maṭha

# Preface

For many years, in the course of my travels and discourses I have repeatedly been requested to compile a simple book to address our basic teachings in an accessible manner for aspiring students. While I feel most unqualified for such an undertaking, due to the sincere request of the Vaiṣṇavas I felt duty-bound to take up this task.

What follows are the teachings of our *sampradāya* (lineage) as I have heard them from my spiritual master, His Divine Grace Śrīla Bhakti Pramode Purī Gosvāmī Ṭhākura, our *śāstra*, and our *guru-varga*. I have endeavored to faithfully represent our *siddhānta* without changing or concocting any point contained herein.

In today's world it has become commonplace that many basic points of philosophy are being debated that were never in contention at the time of His Divine Grace Śrīla Prabhupāda Bhaktisiddhānta Sarasvatī Gosvāmī Ṭhākura when he founded the Gauḍīya Maṭha, or His Divine Grace Śrīla Saccidānanda Bhaktivinoda Ṭhākura, discoverer of Lord Caitanya's birthplace (Yoga-pīṭha temple), in his many writings and publications.

It is distressing to see that in such a short time after their disappearance from this world so much understanding about the nature of the *jīva*, *guru-tattva*, the practice of *sādhana*, and Vaiṣṇava etiquette, as well as many other foundational teachings, has become adulterated by misconception and manipulation.

It is the right of every *jīva* to know the truth from a bona fide disciplic succession. We are all fortunate to be connected to such a distinguished line of spiritual preceptors, whose qualifications are indisputable and extraordinary.

I pray that in my humble effort to serve their mission through this publication I have not made any mistake or offense.

With folded palms,
*dāsānudāsa* B. B. Bodhāyan

# I

# The Soul and God

## 1
## Who are we?

According to Vedic wisdom, we are conscious living entities known as *jīvas*. We are in possession of a human body, given by the Supreme Lord, which is the best type of body for developing spiritual understanding. But we are not the material body. We are spirit soul.

## 2
## What is the true identity of the *jīva*?

Although we can see that there are various types of material bodies, such as the human body, animals, birds, insects, and so on, our true identity has nothing to do with these temporary bodies. These bodies are only vehicles for the *jīva*.

The *jīva's* constitutional function is to serve the Supreme Lord Śrī Kṛṣṇa as His eternal servant in pure unconditional love. The *jīva*, having forgotten its constitutional function, has entered into *saṁsāra* (the cycle of birth and death) and is transmigrating from one type of body to another, with the possibility of experiencing 8,400,000 different life forms, according to the laws of *karma*. In this material state of existence, he is suffering and enjoying, but the *jīva's* true happiness is found when he reestablishes his eternal relation with the Supreme Lord, Śrī Kṛṣṇa.

## 3
## Who is the Supreme Lord of all creation?

In *Śrī Brahmā Saṁhitā,* Lord Brahmā has taught that Śrī Kṛṣṇa is the Supreme Lord, both the origin and the cause of all existence. Kṛṣṇa existed before the creation of the universe, Kṛṣṇa exists in the present, and Kṛṣṇa will continue to exist after the destruction of the universe. However, to give pleasure to His devotees who desire to relish relations of parental love with Him, He takes birth in this world from time to time. For example, in Dvāpara-yuga (Bronze Age) Kṛṣṇa appeared as the son of Nanda Mahārāja and Yaśodā Devī, and in doing so He reciprocated with their loving sentiments of parental love. He appeared in an area of Vṛndāvana known as Gokula. The residents of Vṛndāvana, known as the *vrajavāsīs*, lovingly called Him Govinda. The Supreme Lord of the entire universe is Śrī Kṛṣṇa, also known as Govinda ("He who gives pleasure to the cows"). This is exhaustively explained in *Śrī Brahmā Saṁhitā:*

*eko 'py asau racayituṁ jagad-aṇḍa-koṭiṁ*
*yac-chaktir asti jagad-aṇḍa-cayā yad-antaḥ*
*aṇḍāntara-stha-paramāṇu-cayāntara-stham-*
*govindam ādi-puruṣaṁ tam ahaṁ bhajāmi*

"He is an undifferentiated entity as there is no distinction between potency and the possessor thereof. In His work of creation of millions of worlds, His potency remains inseparable. All the universes exist in Him and He is present in His fullness in every one of the atoms that are scattered throughout the universe, at one and the same time. Such is the primeval Lord Govinda whom I adore." (*Śrī Brahmā Saṁhitā* 5.35)

## 4

## What are the different ages, or *yugas*?

According to the Vedic literature, time in the material universe passes through giant epochs, which can be likened to the seasons which rotate and possess distinctive characteristics. These four ages are Satya-yuga (Golden Age), Tretā-yuga (Silver Age), Dvāpara-yuga (Bronze Age), and Kali-yuga (Iron Age). People of Satya-yuga are characterized by religiosity, virtue, self-control, intelligence, and a long lifespan. Each age progressively degenerates until we reach Kali-yuga, the current age, which is known as an age of irreligiosity, vice, foolishness, quarrel, and hypocrisy. The people of Kali-yuga are plagued by disease and a short lifespan.

## 5

## In this age of Kali-yuga, characterized by constant quarrel and hypocrisy, how can we reach Kṛṣṇa, the Supreme Lord?

In this crooked age of Kali-yuga, which is full of quarrel and hypocrisy, people have short lives, little intelligence, and are plagued with problems. The Supreme Lord Śrī Kṛṣṇa, out of His causeless compassion for the *jīvas*, has appeared in this world as the holy name—the Hare Kṛṣṇa *mahā-mantra:*

*Hare Kṛṣṇa Hare Kṛṣṇa*
*Kṛṣṇa Kṛṣṇa Hare Hare*
*Hare Rāma Hare Rāma*
*Rāma Rāma Hare Hare*

The Supreme Lord has invested all of His multitude of energies in the Hare Kṛṣṇa *mahā-mantra*. There is no consideration of proper time, place, caste, creed, or condition to remember or to recite the holy names. Śrī Kṛṣṇa has instructed us to remember and chant His names at every single moment. A person can attain the fullest benefit from chanting the Hare Kṛṣṇa *mahā-mantra* when it is accepted from a spiritual master through the process of *dīkṣā* (initiation). An *ācārya,* or the spiritual master, is authorized by the disciplic succession of spiritual masters, the *guru-paramparā*, to give initiation.

He teaches his disciples through his own practice and ideal example. By offering appropriate respect and worship to all the members of the *paramparā* and by chanting the Hare Kṛṣṇa *mahā-mantra* with faith and attention, the *jīvas* of this world will become eternally liberated from this miserable and painful cycle of birth and death. By the process of chanting, the *jīvas* will experience self-realization and bliss. They will gain entrance into the spiritual abode of the Supreme Lord Śrī Kṛṣṇa, known as Goloka Vṛndāvana, by the special mercy of Śrīmatī Rādhārāṇī, *hlādinī-śakti* (the bliss-bestowing potency of the Lord).

## 6

## Where does the *jīvātmā* (atomic individual living entity) come from?

The Supreme Lord is the Supreme Soul, or *paramātmā*. If we imagine the Supreme Soul as being a huge fire, then the individual souls, *jīvātmās*, are the tiny sparks that are expelled from that huge fire. In brief, we can say that Śrī Kṛṣṇa is the main principle of all existence, while the *jīvātmās* are tiny minuscule parts of Him, existing within and depending on Him.

⬦⬦⬦

## 7
## What is the proof that the living entities came from the Supreme Lord?

Once, somebody asked a tree, "What is your identity?" The tree replied, "My identity is revealed by my fruits—*phalena paricīyate.*" Similarly, the Supreme Lord is the tree of all living beings. He is eternally blissful, peaceful, and full of love. Because we are conditioned by the material energy, we are unable to realize the qualities of the purely spiritual Supreme Lord. However, by our very nature, as the fruits of that supreme tree, being parts and parcels of the Lord, we also possess the qualities of bliss, peace, and love in our purified state. The living entities (*jīvas*) are not their material bodies; they are actually souls coming from the *paramātmā* (supersoul). The material bodies are temporary, whereas the souls are eternal. The soul is perpetually going through the cycle of birth and death, attaining new bodies according to the fruits of its actions (*karma-phala*). The Supreme Lord Śrī Kṛṣṇa says in the *Bhagavad-gītā*, "*mamaivāṁśo jīva-loke jīva-bhūtaḥ sanātanaḥ:* All living entities are My separated parts and parcels and they are eternal."

The empirical scientific method is dependent on tangible evidence. With time and advancement in technology, some of their ideas and theories must be altered or changed. Ideas that are subject to change are not permanent, and that which is not permanent cannot be totally reliable.

The theory of evolution is a hotly debated topic, much talked about in both religious and scientific circles. The word "theory" should be noted strongly here. Although some evidence was found, the subject matter is still based on a "theory" and, as a result, should not be taken as fact. There are areas within the theory, such as transmutation, that are controversial, even among some biologists. So, although science is trying to make sense of the world around us, it is not without controversies, debates, and uncertainties. It is also worth noting here that science has a muddy idea on the origin of life. There are scientific theories that life began as single-celled microorganisms some billions of years ago, and also that humans have evolved from primates and that we share a common ancestry.

As for our line of spirituality, we do not believe that we have evolved either from microorganisms or primates, nor do we believe that we share common ancestors with them. According to the Vedic scriptures, we humans are the direct descendants of Manu, who was the first human being and the son of Lord Brahmā.

The knowledge we have received is unchanged, unmodified, and completely perfect because it is coming down from the perfect person, Lord Kṛṣṇa. This knowledge is eternal and is taken as the ultimate fact. It is truth without debate.

## 8

## Nowadays, there is some controversy about whether it is possible for the *jīva* to fall down from Vaikuṇṭha/Goloka

to become bound again in the material world. How should we understand this according to the revealed scriptures?

Śrī Kṛṣṇa says in the *Bhagavad-gītā* (15.6):

*na tad bhāsayate sūryo*
*na śaśāṅko na pāvakaḥ*
*yad gatvā na nivartante*
*tad dhāma paramaṁ mama*

One who has reached My eternal abode, Goloka-dhāma, never has to come back to the material world of death.

Then again, Śrī Kṛṣṇa says elsewhere in the *Bhagavad-gītā* (8.16):

*ā-brahma-bhuvanāl lokāḥ*
*punar āvartino 'rjuna*
*mām upetya tu kaunteya*
*punar janma na vidyate*

Śrī Kṛṣṇa is explaining, "O Arjuna, I am beyond the influence of time. These fourteen worlds are bound by time. The living entities in the material world must take birth again and again, even if they reach the highest planet of Lord Brahmā. But on reaching My eternal abode or on reaching Me, the souls never have to take birth again in this material world of death."

We have now heard the above two opinions directly spoken from the lotus mouth of the Supreme Lord. Thus, how can we possibly believe that this type of baseless mental concoction about the soul falling down from the spiritual world is authorized by the revealed scriptures?

The revealed scriptures describe the soul as being *taṭasthā-śakti,* which means it is situated on the border (*taṭa*). This implies that it is not dull matter nor is it the supreme spiritual substance but it exists somewhere between the two. When it maintains an intimate connection with matter it is called a *baddha-jīva* (a soul that is bound), and when it is free from the influence of matter and established in its constitutional spiritual position it is called *nitya-mukta* (eternally liberated). Association with people established in the absolute truth (*sādhu-saṅga*) enables the soul to attain its eternal constitutional position. On gaining its eternal spiritual form, the soul goes to the Supreme Lord, either in Goloka or Vaikuṇṭha.

However, since the topic has arisen, we must see what the secret is behind it. We know the following from *Śrī Caitanya-caritāmṛta* (*Ādi-līlā* 5.65):

*dūra haite puruṣa kare māyāte avadhāna*
*jīva-rūpa vīrya tāte karena ādhāna*

> The first *puruṣa* casts His glance at *māyā* from a distance, and thus He impregnates her with the seed of life in the form of the living entities.

The Supreme Lord has placed the *jīva* in the border region (*taṭa*). The border is the region where the material world and the spiritual world meet. In their current state they are neither purely spiritual nor purely material but are a soul encased in a material body. If we consider the words of *Śrī Caitanya-caritāmṛta*, we can come to the conclusion that the *jīvas* were all present within the Supreme Lord in the form of seeds. These *jīvas* will gain the right to enter the spiritual world when they attain their eternal constitutional position by worshiping the Supreme Lord. This is why our previous spiritual masters have exclaimed, "Everyone is situated in Goloka in their eternal constitutional position—*svarūpe sabāra haya golokete sthiti.*" This means that until the *jīvas* realize their eternal position as being eternal servants of the Supreme Lord, they cannot exist in their eternal spiritual form in Goloka. If this eternal spiritual form is once realized, then the *jīva* never comes back to this world of death and material attachments, unless it is on the desire of the Supreme Lord to assist in His pastimes. For example, Śrī Kṛṣṇa Caitanya Mahāprabhu is Śrī Kṛṣṇa Himself, who came to the material world along with His associates to deliver the fallen souls. The associates of Śrī Caitanya Mahāprabhu were simultaneously present in Goloka Vṛndāvana as well as in the material world. In Goloka-dhāma they were engaged in the eternal service of the Supreme Lord, and they also appeared in the material world to serve the Supreme Lord Śrī Kṛṣṇa Caitanya Mahāprabhu in His pastimes.

The *jīva,* due to the influence of *māyā* (illusion), has forgotten his eternal relation with the Lord, even though the Lord is the seed-giving father of his very existence. An analogy may be used to help clarify this point. Suppose that a man goes to a foreign country and somehow establishes intimate relations with a local woman and she becomes pregnant. Shortly afterwards, the man returns home and does not return. Twenty years later, the child cherishes a desire to know who his father is. He may think, "Only my mother can give me genuine information about my father." In this way, at twenty years of age, the child asks his mother about his father, and she tells all about him. After hearing of his father's residence in another country, the child endeavors to ready himself to travel and visit him.

He arranges a passport, visa, and a plane ticket and flies to that other country, where he meets his father. So, originally the child was in his father's country in the form of a seed. However, the child's father implanted that seed in the mother's country and then went back to his own country. The passport, visa, and plane ticket can be seen to represent the spiritual practice (*sādhana*) of the child through which he was able to meet his father. Therefore, while in the border region (*taṭa*), when under the influence of *māyā* (material illusion), we have forgotten our relation to the Supreme Lord and have been wandering in the material world birth after birth as a result. Now, due to the association of true seekers of the absolute truth (*sādhu-saṅga*) and through chanting *harināma* (the holy name) under the guidance of an authorized guru, we can become qualified to return to our father, Śrī Kṛṣṇa. Once we reach our father, He will never let us fall back again into this material world of birth and death.

## 9
## Can the living entity ever become the Supreme Lord?

The *jīvas* are the eternal servants of the Supreme Lord, and the nature of a servant is to always serve the master. Therefore the *jīva* can never become the Supreme Lord.

## 10

## Who can we understand to be the Supreme Lord? How is He different from others?

That person in whom the six qualities are manifest in their entirety is known as Bhagavān, or the Supreme Lord.

As stated in the *Viṣṇu Purāṇa* (6.5.47):

*aiśvaryasya samagrasya vīryasya yaśasaḥ śriyaḥ*
*jñāna-vairāgyayoś caiva ṣaṇṇāṁ bhaga itīṅganā*

> One who is complete in the six opulences of wealth, power, fame, beauty, knowledge, and renunciation is known as Bhagavān.

## 11

## Who possesses these six qualities in their highest degree?

Lord Kṛṣṇa is the only person who is in full

possession of all these six qualities to their superlative degree. He is called *līlā-puruṣottama,* the Lord of wonderful pastimes, who appeared as the son of Nanda Mahārāja (Nanda-nandana) and Yaśodā Devī (Yaśodā-nandana) in Dvāpara-yuga. He is the origin of all and the *avatārī* (original source) of all *avatāra*s (divine incarnations).

## 12

## What does the word *avatārī* mean?

The Lord appears in many *avatāra* forms, such as *puruṣa-avatāra, līlā-avatāra, guṇa-avatāra, manvantara-avatāra, yuga-avatāra,* and *śaktyāveśa-avatāra.* All these *avatāra*s serve various functions. When *dharma* is under immense threat and almost lost, they become manifest for the purpose of reinstating *dharma.* They attract the *jīvātmās* back to their original constitutional position by their various wonderful *līlās* (pastimes), and through spiritual teachings they reestablish *dharma* for the upliftment of the *jīvas.* Although each is unique in character, they all originate from Lord Kṛṣṇa. Therefore, being the source of all incarnations, He is known as *avatārī.*

## 13
## What are the different types of *avatāras*?

There are six types of *avatāras* (with examples of each):

(1) *Puruṣa-avatāra* - Originating from Saṅkarṣaṇa and involved in the creation and maintenance of the material worlds, the three *puruṣa-avatāras* are:
   (a) Kāraṇodakaśāyī Viṣṇu (residing on the Causal Ocean)
   (b) Garbhodakaśāyī Viṣṇu (residing on the Garbhodaka Ocean)
   (c) Kṣīrodakaśāyī Viṣṇu (residing on the Ocean of Milk and within the heart of all living entities)

(2) *Līlā-avatāra:* Matsya, Kūrma, Varāha, Narasiṁha, Vāmana, Bhṛgupati, Rāma, Balarāma, Buddha, and Kalki

(3) *Guṇa-avatāra:*
   (a) Mahā-Viṣṇu: incarnation of the mode of goodness (*sattva-guṇa*)

- (b) Brahmā: incarnation of the mode of passion (*rajo-guṇa*)
- (c) Śiva: incarnation of the mode of ignorance (*tamo-guṇa*)

(4) *Manvantara-avatāra:* Yajña, Vibhu, Satyasena, Hari, Vaikuṇṭha, Ajita, Vāmana, Sārvabhauma, Ṛṣabhadeva, Viṣvaksena, Dharmasetu, Sudāmā, Yogeśvara, and Bṛhadbhānu

(5) *Yuga-avatāra:* appear in each of the four *yugas* as *śukla* (white) in Satya-yuga, *rakta* (red) in Tretā-yuga, *kṛṣṇa* (black) in Dvāpara-yuga, and *pīta* (yellow) in Kali-yuga

(6) *Śaktyāveśa-avatāra:* Pṛthu, Vyāsa, Paraśurāma, Buddha

## 14
## Is Śrī Caitanya (Gaurāṅga) Mahāprabhu God?

Yes. The most munificent and magnanimous form of Śrī Kṛṣṇa is Śrī Caitanya Mahāprabhu. The Supreme Lord took the form of Śrī Caitanya Mahāprabhu to distribute divine love and is therefore known as *prema-puruṣottama*. Śrī Kṛṣṇa and Caitanya Mahāprabhu are one and the same. Caitanya Mahāprabhu cannot be called an *avatāra* of Śrī Kṛṣṇa. He is Śrī Kṛṣṇa Himself—not an expansion like other *avatāras*. Śrī Kṛṣṇa is the source of all incarnations (*avatārī*) and came as Caitanya Gosāi (Śrī Kṛṣṇa Caitanya Mahāprabhu). The Supreme Lord of pastimes (*līlā-puruṣottama*), Śrī Kṛṣṇa, who appeared in Dvāpara-yuga, again appeared in Kali-yuga as the Supreme Lord to bestow divine love (*prema-puruṣottama*).

# II

# Guru Parampara

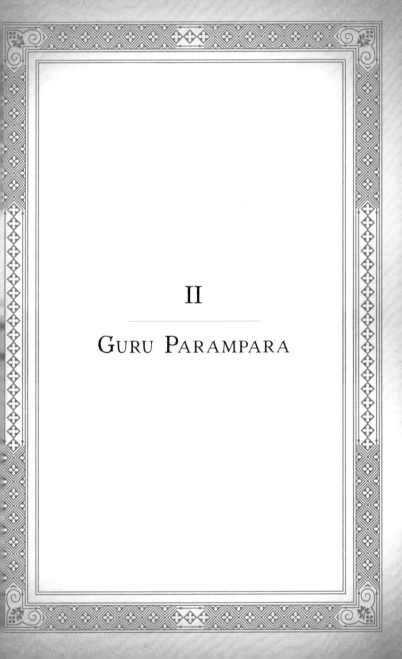

## 15
## What does the word *paramparā*, or *sampradāya*, mean?

Those who follow the principles of pure devotion as prescribed by the Supreme Lord, Śrī Kṛṣṇa, and His incarnations are known to belong to a system called a *paramparā* or *sampradāya*. It implies an unbroken lineage of teachers (gurus) and disciples (*śiṣyas*).

## 16
## What is the name of the *dharma* (spiritual principles and practices) that we follow?

In a broad sense, the *dharma* we are following is known as *vaiṣṇava-dharma*. *Vaiṣṇava-dharma* implies the reestablishing of our long-lost relationship with the Supreme Lord by rendering favorable loving devotional service to Him. Although there are different Vaiṣṇava practices in India, those who follow Śrī Caitanya Mahāprabhu desire to establish loving devotion to Śrī Kṛṣṇa in the mood of the *gopīs*, headed by His bliss-bestowing potency, Śrīmatī Rādhārāṇī.

Only by the mercy of Śrīmatī Rādhārāṇī can one gain access to the service of the Lord.

## 17
## Who is Rādhārāṇī? What is Her significance?

First of all, we have to know the meaning of the name Rādhā. The verb *rādh* means "to be satisfied" or "to perfectly bestow bliss." She who bestows pure love upon Śrī Kṛṣṇa in the most excellent manner is Śrīmatī Rādhārāṇī. There is no difference between Rādhā and Kṛṣṇa. As stated in *Śrī Caitanya-caritāmṛta* (*Ādi-līlā* 4.96):

*rādhā—pūrṇa-śakti, kṛṣṇa—pūrṇa-śaktimān*
*dui vastu bheda nāi, śāstra-paramāṇa*

Śrī Rādhā is the complete energy of the completely energetic person, Śrī Kṛṣṇa. There is no difference between the two of Them. This is proven by the revealed scriptures.

According to the information from our previous teachers, Rādhā is the pleasure potency of Śrī Kṛṣṇa. Kṛṣṇa is the object of our service, but He accepts all service through Rādhārāṇī. Also, in the *Nārada Purāṇa*, Kṛṣṇa makes the following declaration:

*satyaṁ satyaṁ punaḥ satyaṁ*
*satyaṁ satyaṁ punaḥ punaḥ*
*vinā rādhā prasādena*
*mat-prasado na vidyate*

"It is the truth! It is the truth! It is the truth! I declare it again and again. Without the mercy of Rādhā My mercy does not manifest."

An *ācārya* is also one who teaches us how to serve Kṛṣṇa in the most precious manner. Thus we can come to the conclusion that Rādhārāṇī is the ultimate *ācārya* of our lineage. Whoever has been selected by the previous teachers in our lineage to become an initiating guru is a representative of Śrīmatī Rādhārāṇī.

## 18
## How many *sampradāyas* are present in *vaiṣṇava-dharma*?

Śrī Caitanya, who is the most munificent and magnanimous form of Śrī Kṛṣṇa, taught us that there are four Vaiṣṇava *sampradāyas*.

## 19
## What are the names of the four Vaiṣṇava *sampradāyas*?

(1) Śrī-sampradāya
(2) Brahma-sampradāya
(3) Rudra-sampradāya
(4) Sanaka-sampradāya

# 20
# Did the practice of the Vaiṣṇava *sampradāyas* start spreading only from the time of Śrī Caitanya?

Vaiṣṇava *sampradāyas* began from the time of the creation of the universe. Śrī Balarāma is the cause of the creation of this universe. In Śrī Kṛṣṇa's pastimes, Balarāma appears as His older brother. He is an expansion of Śrī Kṛṣṇa's internal potency (*svarūpa-śakti*) and is also known as Mūla-Saṅkarṣaṇa. Balarāma manifests in five different forms to serve Śrī Kṛṣṇa: Kāraṇodakaśāyī Mahā-viṣṇu, Garbhodakaśāyī Viṣṇu, Kṣīrodakaśāyī Viṣṇu, Saṅkarṣaṇa, and Śeṣa. Kāraṇodakaśāyī Mahā-Viṣṇu creates the universe. In order to create the *jīvas* He takes on the form of Garbhodakaśāyī Viṣṇu. A lotus flower sprouts from the navel of Garbhodakaśāyī Viṣṇu, and within the stem of that lotus all the fourteen planetary systems exist (*caturdaśa-bhuvana*).

The top of the lotus stem sprouts a lotus flower from which Lord Brahmā, the first *jīva,* is automatically manifested by the Lord's desire. This Brahmā was a Vaiṣṇava. We are descending from the *paramparā* of that same Lord Brahmā, born from the lotus flower. In this way, the Vaiṣṇava *sampradāyas'* origins can be traced back right to the beginning of creation.

## 21

## What are the names of the main *ācāryas* of each of the four *sampradāyas,* and who appointed those individuals to be *ācāryas*?

(1) Śrī-sampradāya:
"Śrī" refers to Lakṣmī Devī. She is the potency of Lord Nārāyaṇa and is the expansion of His opulence. Lakṣmī Devī appointed Rāmānuja as the *ācārya* of the Śrī-sampradāya.

(2) Brahma-sampradāya:
Lord Brahmā is the secondary universal creator; he creates the various species of life that the *jīvas* incarnate into. Lord Brahmā is the manifestation of Śrī Kṛṣṇa in the mode of passion (*rajo-guṇa-avatāra*). Lord Brahmā appointed Madhvācārya as the *ācārya* of the Brahma-sampradāya.

(3) Rudra-sampradāya:
Rudra, or Lord Śiva, is the destroyer of the created universe. Lord Siva is a manifestation of Śrī Kṛṣṇa in the mode of ignorance (*tamo-guṇa-avatāra*). Lord Śiva appointed Viṣṇusvāmī as the *ācārya* of the Rudra-sampradāya.

(4) Sanaka-sampradāya:
The four Kumāras were born from Lord Brahmā's mind. They are called Sanaka, Sanātana, Sanandana, and Sanāt-kumāra. In Satya-yuga, a *brāhmaṇa* named Nimbāditya was ordered by Lord Śiva to approach the four Kumāras to receive *dīkṣā* (initiation into divine *mantras*). After receiving initiation, Nimbāditya meditated on the Supreme Lord Śrī Kṛṣṇa. Being pleased with Nimbāditya, Śrī Kṛṣṇa revealed Himself to him in the form of Gaurāṅga Mahāprabhu and said, "In Kali-yuga, you will be born as a proud scholar named Keśava Kāśmīrī. As a young boy I will defeat you in debate, thereby completely crushing your pride. From then onward you will become My devotee and you will be known as Nimbārkācārya." In this way, by the strength of the mercy of Bhagavān, the four Kumāras appointed Nimbārkācārya as the *ācārya* of the Sanaka-sampradāya.

## 22
## Which *sampradāya* are the Gauḍīya Vaiṣṇavas a part of?

We are disciples and grand-disciples of he who has entered the Lord's eternal pastimes (*nitya-līlā-praviṣṭa*), the founder of Śrī Gopīnātha Gauḍīya Maṭha, the living example of the verse, *tṛṇād api su-nīcena,* Śrīla Bhakti Pramode Purī Gosvāmī Ṭhākura. Śrīla Bhakti Pramode Purī Gosvāmī Ṭhākura was one of the prominent disciples of Śrīla Prabhupāda Bhaktisiddhānta Sarasvatī Ṭhākura, who was the sole disciple of Śrīla Gaurakiśora dāsa Bābājī Mahārāja. Śrīla Prabhupāda was the son of Saccidānanda Bhaktivinoda Ṭhākura Mahāśaya. We are part of the Brahma-sampradāya, in the family of Advaita Ācārya, through the line of his son, Kṛṣṇa Miśra.

# *Guru Parampara*

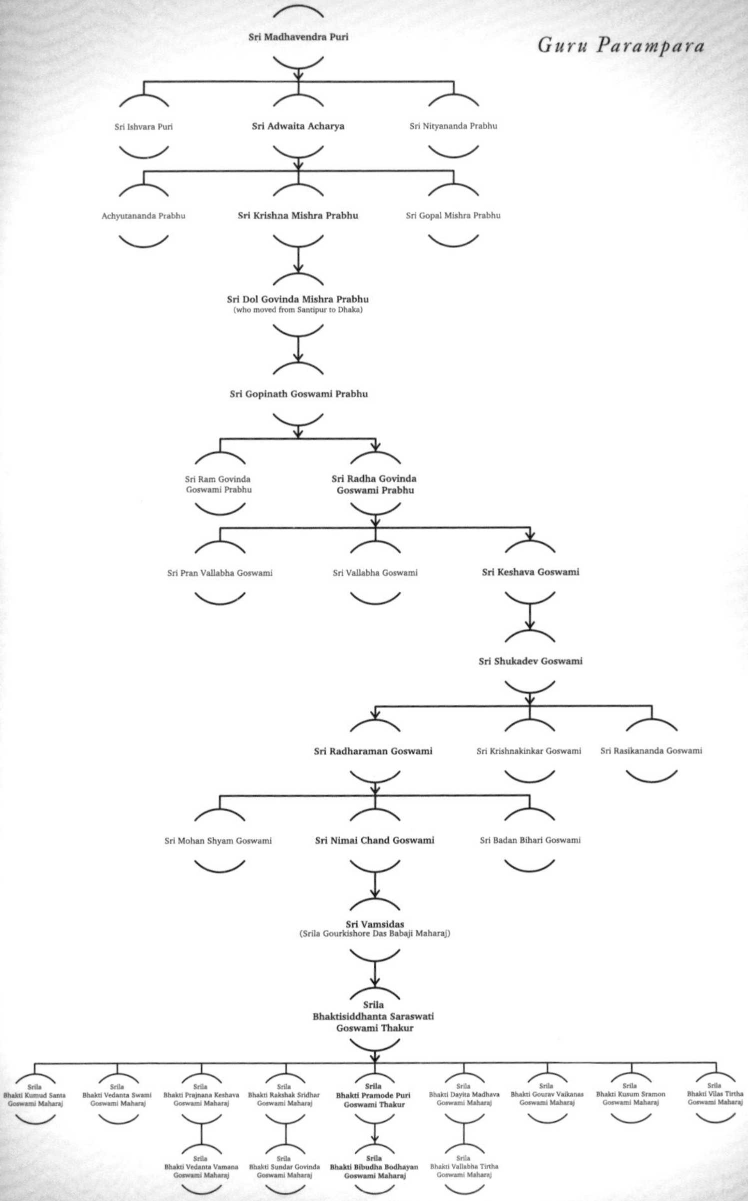
Sri Madhavendra Puri
Sri Ishvara Puri
Sri Adwaita Acharya
Sri Nityananda Prabhu
Achyutananda Prabhu
Sri Krishna Mishra Prabhu
Sri Gopal Mishra Prabhu
Sri Dol Govinda Mishra Prabhu
(who moved from Santipur to Dhaka)
Sri Gopinath Goswami Prabhu
Sri Ram Govinda Goswami Prabhu
Sri Radha Govinda Goswami Prabhu
Sri Pran Vallabha Goswami
Sri Vallabha Goswami
Sri Keshava Goswami
Sri Shukadev Goswami
Sri Radharaman Goswami
Sri Krishnakinkar Goswami
Sri Rasikananda Goswami
Sri Mohan Shyam Goswami
Sri Nimai Chand Goswami
Sri Badan Bihari Goswami
Sri Vamsidas
(Srila Gourkishore Das Babaji Maharaj)
Srila Bhaktisiddhanta Saraswati Goswami Thakur
Srila Bhakti Kumud Santa Goswami Maharaj
Srila Bhakti Vedanta Swami Goswami Maharaj
Srila Bhakti Prajnana Keshava Goswami Maharaj
Srila Bhakti Rakshak Sridhar Goswami Maharaj
Srila Bhakti Pramode Puri Goswami Thakur
Srila Bhakti Dayita Madhava Goswami Maharaj
Srila Bhakti Gourav Vaikanas Goswami Maharaj
Srila Bhakti Kusum Sramon Goswami Maharaj
Srila Bhakti Vilas Tirtha Goswami Maharaj
Srila Bhakti Vedanta Vamana Goswami Maharaj
Srila Bhakti Sundar Govinda Goswami Maharaj
Srila Bhakti Bibudha Bodhayan Goswami Maharaj
Srila Bhakti Vallabha Tirtha Goswami Maharaj

## 23
## What is the name of the founder of the Sārasvata Gauḍīya-sampradāya?

The founder of Śrī Gauḍīya Maṭha is one who has entered the Lord's eternal pastimes (*nitya-līlā-praviṣṭa*), Śrī Śrīla Prabhupāda Bhaktisiddhānta Sarasvatī Gosvāmī Ṭhākura, referred to by many as Śrīla Prabhupāda.

## 24
## What austerities did Śrīla Prabhupāda perform before preaching Śrīmān Mahāprabhu's message of loving devotion?

Before undertaking the task of spreading Śrīmān Mahāprabhu's message, Śrīla Prabhupāda completed a vow of chanting one billion names of Lord Kṛṣṇa. Śrīla Prabhupāda chanted 300,000 names of Lord Kṛṣṇa (192 rounds) daily on his chanting beads, following in the footsteps of Nāmācārya Śrīla Haridāsa Ṭhākura, who was the living example of chanting the Hare Kṛṣṇa *mahā-mantra*. Through completing this great vow he gained the strength to spread Caitanya Mahāprabhu's message of divine loving devotion all over the world.

## 25
## What was Śrīla Prabhupāda Bhaktisiddhānta Sarasvatī Ṭhākura thinking about while performing this austerity of chanting one billion names of the Lord, and why?

Within the first year of Śrīla Prabhupāda's vow, his two great gurus, Śrīla Bhaktivinoda Ṭhākura and Śrīla Gaurakiśora dāsa Bābājī Mahārāja, manifested their disappearance pastimes. Śrīla Bhaktivinoda Ṭhākura manifested his disappearance pastime in 1914 (Bengali date: 9th Āṣāḍha 1321), and Śrīla Gaurakiśora dāsa Bābājī Mahārāja manifested his disappearance pastime on the day of Utthāna Ekādaśī (19th November, 1915). Consequently, Śrīla Prabhupāda thought, "The goal of preaching is to bestow auspiciousness on the souls of this world. These two divine personalities have left and have made it impossible for the worldly souls to directly take shelter of their lotus feet. What will I achieve by preaching now, in the face of these circumstances?

"The conditioned souls are afflicted by the pain of a multitude of sufferings in this material world; but now, to whose divine lotus feet will I take these souls? I myself have lost my divine shelter, and now these souls have also lost their shelter. The Hare Kṛṣṇa *mahā-mantra* is the one and only hope in this Kali-yuga. Therefore I will spend the rest of my life just as Haridāsa Ṭhākura did, chanting 300,000 holy names daily. What will be the gain if I now begin preaching Śrīman Mahāprabhu's message of divine love?"

## 26
## Who changed Śrīla Prabhupāda Bhaktisiddhānta Sarasvatī Gosvāmī

Ṭhākura's mind? Who inspired him to push on and preach the message of Śrī Caitanya?

Śrīla Prabhupāda Bhaktisiddhānta Sarasvatī Gosvāmī Ṭhākura was known as Bimala Prasāda at that time. Śrīmān Mahāprabhu's supreme desire was to bestow auspiciousness on the residents of this world through Bimala Prasāda. One day, during the auspicious *brāhma-muhūrta* (roughly ninety minutes before sunrise), the Pañca-tattva—Śrī Caitanya Mahāprabhu, Śrī Nityānanda Prabhu, Śrī Advaita Ācārya, Śrī Gadādhara Paṇḍita, and Śrī Śrīvāsa Ṭhākura—along with the Six Gosvāmīs—Śrī Rupa, Śrī Sanātana, Śrī Raghunātha Bhatta, Śrī Jīva, Śrī Gopāla Bhaṭṭa, and Śrī Raghunātha Dāsa—as well as Śrīla Bhaktivinoda Ṭhākura and Bimala Prasāda's *gurudeva*, Śrīla Gaurakiśora dāsa Bābājī Mahārāja, appeared before Bimala Prasāda in a divine vision.

They began to instruct him as follows: "Bimala Prasāda, adjust your current mindset. On the completion of your vow you must begin full-scale preaching of pure love for Lord Kṛṣṇa through the distribution of the Hare Kṛṣṇa *mahā-mantra*."

Bimala Prasāda's eyes were streaming with tears, so much so that his chest become drenched. With utmost humility Bimala Prasāda asked, "O dear masters, to preach and expand on a large scale, men and money are extremely important. Where will the manpower and money come from?" On hearing Bimala Prasāda's logical question, all of the members of the *guru-paramparā* spoke in unison: "We will personally send all the men and money that you will need." On speaking these words, the entire *guru-paramparā* disappeared from his vision. After this incident, Bimala Prasāda resolved to preach and distribute the Hare Kṛṣṇa *mahā-mantra* with full conviction.

## 27

## Who did the Lord and the *guru-paramparā* send to assist Bimala Prasāda in the immense task of spreading and preaching of the Hare Kṛṣṇa *mahā-mantra*?

(1) Kuñjābihārī Vidyābhūṣana – later known as Bhakti Vilās Tīrtha Gosvāmī Mahārāja

(2) Vinoda Bihārī Prabhu – later known as Bhakti Prajñāna Keśava Gosvāmī Mahārāja

(3) Pramode Bhushan Chakrabarty – later known as Bhakti Pramode Purī Gosvāmī Ṭhākura

(4) Ramendra Chandra Bhattacharya – later known as Bhakti Rakshak Śrīdhardev Gosvāmī Mahārāja

(5) Abhay Charan De – later known as Bhakti Vedanta Svāmī (most commonly known as Śrīla Prabhupāda around the world)

(6) Hemambar Kumar Bandopadhyay – later known as Bhakti Dayitā Mādhava Mahārāja

(7) Śrī Atul Chandra Bandopadhyay – later known as Bhakti Sāraṅga Gosvāmī Mahārāja

(8) Ujjwaleshwar Rath – later known as Bhakti Gaurav Vaikhānas Gosvāmī Mahārāja

(9) Śrī Ramendranath Mukhopadhyay – later known as Bhakti Hrdoy Bon Mahārāja

(10) Śrī Narasiṁha Pattanayak – later known as Bhakti Vaibhav Purī Gosvāmī Mahārāja

(11) Radharaman Roy – later known as Bhakti Kumud Sant Gosvāmī Mahārāja

## 28
## What does "Śrīla Prabhupāda" mean?

Śrīla Prabhupāda is a title that can be used for a follower of pure devotional service (*śuddha-bhakti*). "Śrīla" is an honorific title used for one who follows the process of pure devotional service under the guidance of the succession of spiritual masters. Such a person should have pure devotion established in his heart. The word *prabhupāda* has two parts, *prabhu* and *pada*. *Prabhu* is referring to Śrīmān Caitanya Mahāprabhu, and *pada* refers to the lotus feet of Mahāprabhu. Personalities who are practicing pure devotional service and following the loving mission of Caitanya Mahāprabhu are eligible to use this title.

## 29
## What qualifies one to be considered a member of the Gauḍīya Vaiṣṇava *sampradāya*?

The Hare Kṛṣṇa *mahā-mantra* is a transcendental vibration coming from Goloka Vṛndāvana. It is not a mundane sound. The *mahā-mantra* is a manifestation of the divine love that is found in Goloka Vṛndāvana, where Śrī Śrī Rādhā and Kṛṣṇa are eternally performing their pastimes. Śrī Kṛṣṇa took on the mood and outward complexion of Śrīmatī Rādhārāṇī and descended to this world as Śrī Kṛṣṇa Caitanya. Śrī Caitanya came to give what was never before given to the people of this world—the knowledge of pure love for Śrī Śrī Rādhā-Kṛṣṇa and the method by which one can develop such pure divine love. Śrī Caitanya distributed this rare knowledge freely, without discrimination. Those individuals who practice the process of *bhakti* (devotion) characterized by *śaraṇāgati* (surrender), as taught by Śrī Caitanya, are considered members of the succession of devotees serving under the guidance of Śrī Caitanya and the other members of the Pañca-tattva. The degree of one's surrender determines how much one is truly part of the Gauḍīya Vaiṣṇava *sampradāya*.

## 30
## What is *śaraṇāgati* (surrender)?

There are six characteristics of surrender:

(1) Humility

(2) Completely offering one's very existence to Śrī Śrī Rādhā-Kṛṣṇa

(3) Keeping faith that Śrī Kṛṣṇa is the sole maintainer of every single *jīva*

(4) Having complete faith that Śrī Kṛṣṇa is one's sole protector

(5) Following that which is favorable for the practice of loving devotion, without any debate

(6) Immediately giving up that which is unfavorable for the practice of loving devotion

All surrendered devotees follow these six characteristics. The pure devotees in the form of gurus and Vaiṣṇavas teach us the process of surrender by their own example. They are the pure representatives of Śrī Śrī Rādhā-Kṛṣṇa. To practice surrender means to follow in the footsteps of the pure devotees and live our lives according to their instructions.

## 31
## How was the title "Śrīla Prabhupāda" conferred on Bimala Prasāda?

In 1918 Bimala Prasāda completed his vow of chanting one billion holy names. The entire society of scholarly Vaiṣṇavas acknowledged Bimala Prasāda's intense dedication to and adoration for the chanting of the Hare Kṛṣṇa *mahā-mantra*. Seeing that Bimala Prasāda possessed all the qualifications and attributes befitting the title, the community of scholarly Vaiṣṇavas conferred on him the honorary title "Śrīla Prabhupāda."

## 32
## Are all preachers qualified to use the title "Śrīla Prabhupāda"?

Those who apply the teachings of surrender as taught by Śrī Kṛṣṇa Caitanya Mahāprabhu, who are endowed with saintliness, and who preach the divine message of loving devotion are qualified to use the title of "Śrīla Prabhupāda."

## 33
## Śrī Gaurahari and the Pañca-tattva sent various people to help Śrīla Prabhupāda (Bimala Prasāda) in spreading the teachings of divine love and pure devotion. Were those individuals qualified to use the title "Śrīla Prabhupāda"?

They were most certainly qualified to use the title. The ultimate spiritual master is one—the Supreme Lord, Śrī Kṛṣṇa. This is the understanding we have from the scriptures and the *guru-paramparā*. Śrī Kṛṣṇa Caitanya is non-different from Śrī Kṛṣṇa and is also the most magnanimous form of Śrī Kṛṣṇa. Those who follow in the footsteps of Śrī Kṛṣṇa Caitanya by practicing and preaching this message of divine love are all representatives of Kṛṣṇa, or spiritual masters (gurus). All of these representatives are embodiments of humility and do not consider themselves qualified to be representatives of Kṛṣṇa or worthy of the status of a spiritual master. Thus, feeling ashamed to use the title for themselves, they use the honorific title "Śrīla Prabhupāda" to refer to their own respective spiritual masters, whom they worship with the utmost reverence. This is why most of the disciples of Śrīla Prabhupāda Bhaktisiddhānta Sarasvatī Ṭhākura (Bimala Prasāda) addressed him as Śrīla Prabhupāda but did not use the title for themselves.

## 34
## What does Pañca-tattva mean?

The word *pañca* means five and the word *tattva* means truth. *Pañca-tattva* refers to the five aspects or forms of Śrī Kṛṣṇa as represented by the manifestations of Śrī Kṛṣṇa Caitanya, Prabhu Nityānanda, Śrī Advaita, Gadādhara, and Śrīvāsa Ṭhākura.

## 35
## Who are the Pañca-tattva and why did they appear on earth?

Pañca-tattva refers to the five forms of Śrī Kṛṣṇa who appeared in Kali-yuga, five hundred years ago. Śrī Kṛṣṇa Caitanya is the Supreme Lord Himself, Śrī Kṛṣṇa, who appeared assuming the role of a devotee; Śrī Kṛṣṇa's own energy, his *svarūpa-śakti,* Balarāma (Mūla-Saṅkarṣaṇa), appeared as Prabhu Nityānanda; Śrī Kṛṣṇa's *puruṣa-avatāra,* Mahā-Viṣṇu, combined with Śrī Kṛṣṇa's *tamo-guṇa-avatāra,* Śiva, to become Śrī Advaita Prabhu; Śrī Kṛṣṇa's bliss-bestowing potency, Śrīmatī Rādhārāṇī, appeared as Gadādhara Paṇḍita; Śrī Kṛṣṇa's form as a sage is Śrī Nārada. Śrī Nārada appeared as Śrīvāsa Paṇḍita.

The Supreme Lord is eternally the son of Nanda Mahārāja, Nanda-nandana Kṛṣṇa. In this Kali-yuga the living entities quarrel for no reason. Furthermore, they are deceptive and hypocritical. Knowing the state of affairs in Kali-yuga, Śrī

Nanda-nandana Kṛṣṇa appeared in five forms known as the Pañca-tattva. He came to deliver the people of this age and teach them how to serve Lord Kṛṣṇa in a pure and simple manner, without incurring any expense.

Śrī Kṛṣṇa, along with His five forms and the other pure souls who were all completely pure and free of all *anarthas* (impediments), engaged in *saṅkīrtana* (congregational chanting of the holy names) in the house of Śrīvāsa Paṇḍita. In this way, Śrī Kṛṣṇa showed us that one need not worship the Lord with excessive extravagance and expense. Rather, one can serve the Supreme Lord through the congregational chanting of the *mahā-mantra* (*harināma-saṅkīrtana*) and easily be delivered from the ocean of birth and death.

## 36

## Was the founder of the Gauḍīya Maṭha, Śrīla Bhaktisiddhānta Sarasvatī Gosvāmī Ṭhākura Prabhupāda, accepted and authorized to be the spiritual preceptor (*ācārya*) by the *guru-paramparā*?

Yes. Śrīla Prabhupāda was most definitely accepted and authorized by the *paramparā*. That is the only reason why he was engaged in distributing the holy name of Kṛṣṇa, bestowing the topmost mercy on the souls of this world. He accepted those who had no spiritual shelter and instructed them, according to their natures, to either live a renounced life in the *maṭha* (monastery) or to live in family life. He engaged both the residents of the *maṭha* and the householders in the practice of chanting the holy name and the various limbs of devotional service to Lord Kṛṣṇa (*hari-bhajana*).

## 37

## Śrīla Prabhupāda was the founder of all the different branches of Śrī Gauḍīya Maṭha. Those of Śrīla Prabhupāda's disciples who were particularly surrendered to his lotus feet eventually became spiritual masters themselves. Did Śrīla Prabhupāda authorize them to become spiritual masters?

Yes, Śrīla Prabhupāda instructed them to preach in order to deliver the souls of this world from their painful, miserable material condition. Śrīla Prabhupāda has also said in many of his discourses, *āmi kahakeo śiṣya kari nai sakalke guru kariyāchi:* "I have not made anybody my disciple; I have made everybody spiritual masters." In line with these words, Śrīla Prabhupāda's disciples practiced and preached this *vaiṣṇava-dharma* and gave initiation to the suffering souls of this world in order to connect them with the *guru-paramparā* and liberate them from the cycle of birth and death. All such disciples of Śrīla Prabhupāda were indeed authorized by him to become spiritual masters.

## 38

## In the future, is it necessary for the grand-disciples and great-grand-disciples of Śrīla Prabhupāda to be appointed by their respective initiating spiritual masters, authorizing them to give initiation and act as spiritual masters themselves? If they are not appointed by

any spiritual authority and instead become gurus according to their own desires, what will be the destination of their surrendered disciples?

To answer the first part of this question, it is of utmost necessity that a disciple begins giving initiation only after he is appointed by his initiating spiritual master. If a person thinks himself to be a spiritual master, then the person can never be considered a genuine spiritual master. In the words of Śrīla Prabhupāda, if one thinks they are a guru (spiritual master), then in fact they are *goru* (cow). They are not spiritual masters but cows. In other words, they will be but a respectable animal at best.

The second part of this question is regarding the disciples that are surrendered to a spiritual master who is not authorized by the *guru-paramparā*. If these sheltered individuals chant the holy names and follow the path of devotion according to the prescribed rules and regulations, then those disciples will gain pious credits (*puṇya*). They will gain residence in the heavenly planets due to these pious credits. If they are fortunate and do not get involved in offenses against devotees, then in their next lives they could get the opportunity to get shelter at the lotus feet of a spiritual master who is authorized by the *guru-paramparā*.

Subsequently, by chanting the *mahā-mantra*, they can gain the ultimate fruit of chanting, which is divine love for Lord Kṛṣṇa. By surrendering to such a spiritual master, they can then receive their eternal service to Śrī Śrī Rādhā-Govinda in the transcendental spiritual realm of Goloka Vṛndāvana.

## 39

## Can anyone who instructs others about the holy name of Śrī Kṛṣṇa (*yāre dekha, tāre kaha 'kṛṣṇa'-upadeśa / āmāra ājñāya guru hañā tāra' ei deśa*) act as guru?

This verse was spoken by Śrī Kṛṣṇa Caitanya Mahāprabhu in *Śrī Caitanya-caritāmṛta* (*Madhya-līlā* 7.128):

*yāre dekha, tāre kaha 'kṛṣṇa'-upadeśa*
*āmāra ājñāya guru hañā tāra' ei deśa*

"Whomever you see, speak to them about the teachings of Kṛṣṇa. In this way, on My order, become a guru and deliver this country."

Nowadays, most preachers are taking shelter of this verse and becoming busy appointing themselves as initiating spiritual masters and bestowing initiation on spiritual seekers. Rather than following Caitanya Mahāprabhu's instructions, some in the Vaiṣṇava community, in the name of preaching pure *vaiṣṇava-dharma*, are instead misrepresenting the concept of guru as quoted above. By doing so, the Vaiṣṇava community has opened up a marketplace where anyone and everyone can feel competent to become guru. In reality, we have begun disregarding Lord Caitanya's instructions. This is my strong belief.

We must carefully analyze this verse: in what context and to whom did Śrī Caitanya speak? During His travels in South India, Śrī Caitanya Mahāprabhu accepted the invitation of a *brāhmaṇa* named Kūrma. Kūrma bathed Lord Caitanya's feet with utmost care, and he and his family drank the water (*caraṇāmṛta*) used to wash Lord Caitanya's lotus feet. With great care the *brāhmaṇa* served *prasādam* to Mahāprabhu. He and his family honored the remnants of Lord Caitanya's meal, which was like nectar, having directly touched Mahāprabhu's lips (*adharāmṛta prasāda*). When Lord Caitanya asked Kūrma for permission to leave, Kūrma said, "O master, I want to go with You! If You leave, it will be impossible for me to tolerate separation from You." Then Mahāprabhu said:

*prabhu kahe — 'aiche bāt kabhu nā kahibā*
*gṛhe rahi' kṛṣṇa-nāma nirantara laibā*
*yāre dekha, tāre kaha 'kṛṣṇa'-upadeśa*
*āmāra ājñāya guru hañā tāra' ei deśa*

> O *brāhmaṇa*! Staying at home, always chant the holy names of Kṛṣṇa with humility. Preach the holy names of Kṛṣṇa. This is My instruction.
>
> *Śrī-Caitanya-caritāmṛta*
> (*Madhya-līlā* 7.127-28)

Many now say that Mahāprabhu instructed the *brāhmaṇa* Kūrma to become a guru by quoting, *āmāra ājñāya guru hañā tāra' ei deśa* and that therefore, instructing others about the holy names of

Kṛṣṇa automatically makes one a guru. Yes, one does become a guru, but this does not qualify one to become a *dīkṣā-guru* (initiating spiritual master). There are four types of gurus described in the revealed scriptures:

(1) *Vartma-pradarśaka-guru*
(2) *Śikṣā-guru*
(3) *Dīkṣā-guru*
(4) *Caitya-guru*

The person who reveals the path of devotion, or who provides an initial impetus, is known as the *vartma-guru* or the *pradarśaka-guru*. An example is when Cintāmaṇi told Bilvamaṅgala, "If you had as much attachment for the Supreme Lord as you have for me, then you would be able to obtain the Supreme Lord very soon." On hearing these words, Bilvamaṅgala's good intelligence was awakened and he hastily started toward Vṛndāvana.

One who is well acquainted with spiritual knowledge, themselves under the guidance of a *sad-guru*, is a fit person from whom to receive instruction. He is known as a *śikṣā-guru* (instructing spiritual master). The person who formally bestows the *mantra* in one's ear, connecting an individual to the *guru-paramparā,* is known as the *dīkṣā-guru* (initiating spiritual master). The person present in the heart of all living entities, the Supreme Lord in the form of *paramātmā,* and who awakens from within inspiration to seek out and worship the Supreme Lord, is known as the *caitya-guru.*

Śrī Kṛṣṇa Caitanya instructed the *brahmāna* Kūrma to engage in serving Kṛṣṇa (*kṛṣṇa-sevā*) and to preach the glories of Kṛṣṇa (*kṛṣṇa-mahimā-pracāra*). Śrī Caitanya Mahāprabhu never instructed that such preaching automatically qualifies one to become a *dīkṣā-guru.* Rather, a preacher is a teacher and, in that context, is called guru; we can have many such *śikṣā-gurus.* However, the *dīkṣā-guru* must be accepted or appointed by the previous spiritual masters, who come in an unbroken line of spiritual masters and disciples (*guru-paramparā*). Otherwise, the *guru-paramparā* is neglected. Below is an example given to clarify this concept.

A high school has many teachers. However, all of them cannot become the principal. The management of the school chooses the principal. Similarly, our *sampradāya* (succession of spiritual masters and disciples) may have many preachers, but not all of them can become *dīkṣā-gurus,* or initiating spiritual masters. Just as the school management appoints the head, the *guru-paramparā* similarly appoints the *dīkṣā-guru.*

The *dīkṣā-guru* must be completely free of unwanted motives and desires. To be free of unwanted motives and desires means that he must be free of desires for material gain, worship, false prestige, and position. He must be free of the desire to enjoy his senses. He must not commit *vaiṣṇava-aparādha* (offenses to the devotees), *nāma-aparādha* (offenses to the holy names), or *dhāma-aparādha* (offenses to the holy places). In addition, he should not commit *sevā-aparādha* (offenses during worshiping the deity of the Lord).

The *dīkṣā-guru* should also be free from envy, a political mentality, and violence toward other living entities. He should always be engaged in chanting the holy names of Lord Hari. The members of the *guru-paramparā* appoint a Vaiṣṇava devotee to the role of *dīkṣā-guru* because they exhibit all these qualities, are always chanting the *mahā-mantra,* and are free of unwanted desires and motives. In this way the Vaiṣṇava who has been appointed to be the guru by the *guru-paramparā* is the only one who can serve as a *dīkṣā-guru.*

To make this concept clearer, examples in which *dīkṣā-gurus* have been appointed are shown from our own *paramparā:*

Śrīla Prabhupāda Bhaktisiddhānta Sarasvatī Gosvāmī Ṭhākura was officially appointed by the Pañca-tattva, Śrīla Gaurakiśora dāsa Bābājī, Śrīla Bhaktivinoda Ṭhākura, and all the associates of Mahāprabhu. All of the great souls who had shelter at the lotus feet of Śrīla Prabhupāda were free of unwanted motives and desires. They were Śrīla Prabhupāda's spiritual commanders in chief. Therefore Śrīla Prabhupāda often said in his spiritual discourses, "I have not made any disciples. All of these people are qualified to be gurus. I have made only gurus." This is why many of Śrīla Prabhupāda's disciples took on the position of *dīkṣā-guru.*

However, in the time after Śrīla Bhaktisiddhānta Prabhupāda, we see how Prabhupāda's disciples appointed their own successors. Śrīla Bhakti Dayitā Mādhava Gosvāmī Mahārāja appointed Śrīla Bhakti Ballabha Tīrtha Gosvāmī Mahārāja to be the next initiating spiritual master in Śrī Caitanya Gauḍīya Maṭha. Śrīla Bhakti Prajñāna Keśava Gosvāmī Mahārāja appointed Śrīla Bhakti Vedanta Vāmana Gosvāmī Mahārāja to be the next initiating spiritual master in Śrī Devānanda Gauḍīya Maṭha and its branches. Śrīla Bhakti Rakshak Śrīdhardev Gosvāmī Mahārāja appointed Śrīla Bhakti Sundar Govinda Gosvāmī Mahārāja as the next initiating spiritual master in Śrī Caitanya Sārasvata Maṭha. There are many examples of how the disciples of Śrīla Prabhupāda personally appointed the next initiating spiritual master to continue the *guru-paramparā*. I hope that the readers understand this concept and process of appointing the next initiating spiritual master in the *guru-paramparā*.

## 40
## Are we able to know who our *dīkṣā-guru* and *śikṣā-guru* will be?

Our intelligence is a product of the material nature. The spiritual master is of the spiritual nature and transcendentally situated. Therefore it is impossible to understand who one's spiritual master is through the material intelligence. First, in order to know our initiating spiritual master, we must pray from the core of our hearts to Śrī Kṛṣṇa, the ultimate spiritual master of the entire universe. If Śrī Kṛṣṇa is pleased with our prayers, then He will manifest from within our hearts. The identity of our initiating spiritual master will be revealed by the fact that the spiritual master is a genuine representative of Śrī Kṛṣṇa. When we eventually meet that spiritual master, who is Śrī Kṛṣṇa's genuine representative, then we will find that his each and every word is in congruence with the revealed scriptures. Every one of his actions will be done with a scriptural reason, and his association will be blissful at every moment. When the above-mentioned symptoms are realized and experienced, and when we no longer have any doubts, then we must understand that the ultimate spiritual master, Śrī Kṛṣṇa, has sent His representative in the form of this particular spiritual master. Having realized this, with folded palms, one must beg the spiritual master for his shelter and systematically become engaged in the worship of Śrī Kṛṣṇa (*hari-bhajana*) through his guidance.

## 41

## Sometimes preachers representing a society or *maṭha* (temple) preach to people and encourage them to get initiated by a particular spiritual master solely for the purpose of promoting the financial wealth, opulence, and prominence of their institution. What will the disciples of such spiritual masters attain?

In this circumstance, if the agent is a representative of a spiritual master who is a pure devotee, then the disciples can possibly attain auspiciousness. Some false spiritual masters make a show of being spiritually advanced and worthy of worship. Some are just involved in collecting money and managing their societies. Such spiritual masters do not even make time to chant the holy names, and even if they do get the time, they still do not chant the *mahā-mantra*. These people only make a show of being genuine spiritual masters. Therefore, disciples of such so-called gurus can never attain the most auspicious result of chanting the *mahā-mantra,* which is divine love for Śrī Kṛṣṇa. Instead, they only end up collecting *puṇya* (pious results).

By gaining piety, one's material happiness increases, and one begins to think that other Vaiṣṇavas are inferior in comparison to oneself. In this way, if one begins committing offenses to the Vaiṣṇavas, even though continuing to chant the *mahā-mantra,* instead of progressing in true spiritual knowledge and renunciation, one begins manifesting more and more material attachments. These people will be haunted by all kinds of negative thoughts unfavorable for devotion. One may chant the *mahā-mantra* for millions of births under the shelter of such a false spiritual master but will never ever attain service to the divine lotus feet of Śrī Kṛṣṇa.

In contrast, by taking shelter of a spiritual master who is a pure devotee of the Supreme Lord and by chanting the holy names without offenses, one's heart becomes purified and one gradually attains pure love for Śrī Kṛṣṇa. Eventually one enters into the divine spiritual realm of Goloka Vṛndāvana and blissfully attains the ultimate goal of life—eternal service to Śrī Śrī Rādhā-Govinda. When one attains the qualification to serve Śrī Śrī Rādhā-Govinda, then one no longer has to roam the material world in various bodies, suffering various pains, and experiencing the miseries of birth and death.

## 42
## What is the behavior of one who has attained divine love for Śrī Kṛṣṇa?

Persons who have attained divine love will be humble and tolerant. They will not desire material wealth, gain, worship, or position, and they will not be violent or envious toward any living entity. All such negative qualities are destroyed for one who has attained divine love. Such persons never give suffering to others, but offer appropriate devotional respect to everybody. They will always chant the holy names of Kṛṣṇa. By establishing this mood in one's heart and by always chanting the holy names, one enters into the divine realm of Goloka Vṛndāvana under the guidance of the *sakhīs*, and taking on the mood of a *mañjarī* engages eternally in the service of Śrī Śrī Rādhā-Govinda.

## 43

## Nowadays, the *ṛtvik* practice seems to be prevalent. Is this practice authorized?

The *ṛtvik* practice of giving initiation on behalf of the *ācārya* (*dīkṣā-guru*) is authorized only when that *ācārya* is physically present in the material world. The *ācārya* can instruct a person to act as a *ṛtvik* and give initiation into Vaiṣṇava *mantras* once the candidate's suitability for initiation is assessed. This method of the *ṛtvik* practice is authorized. When the *ācārya* completes his pastimes of delivering the conditioned souls in his current body and returns to the eternal spiritual world, Goloka Vṛndāvana, then the *ṛtvik* practice of giving initiation into Vaiṣṇava *mantras* on behalf of that *ācārya* is no longer considered valid.

## 44
## What will be the destination of those getting initiated into a *mantra* through speculative and unauthorized *ṛtvik* practices?

People chanting under the guidance of an unauthorized *ṛtvik* will not be able to achieve the fruit of chanting the *mahā-mantra,* which is attaining divine love for Śrī Kṛṣṇa. Rather than obtaining transcendental love, these people will only obtain more and more material desires and attachments. As long as we maintain attachments to the material world, we will be forced to experience sadness and suffering due to our previous activities and return again and again to this material world in the bodies of various species of life. Intelligent people never consider accepting initiation into a *mantra* through any unauthorized *ṛtvik* process. Wise people call out to Śrī Kṛṣṇa from the core of their heart with the hope to obtain a genuine living spiritual master. Ultimately, Śrī Kṛṣṇa is the guru of the entire world, and at the ripe moment He will send us His pure devotee representative—a genuine spiritual master.

## 45

## The revealed scriptures describe that the spiritual master is non-different from the Supreme Lord. How can this be?

The revealed scriptures state the truth. We are souls filled with unwanted desires and motives. As long as our hearts are filled with these unwanted desires, we will never be able to receive the Supreme Lord's mercy directly. The Supreme Lord, in order to bestow His causeless mercy on the fallen souls, sends us His pure devotees in the form of the spiritual master and the Vaiṣṇavas. In this way, we receive the causeless shower of the Lord's mercy despite having many unwanted motives and desires. This is why the revealed scriptures state that the spiritual master is non-different from the Supreme Lord. Superficially, one may perceive many differences between the Supreme Lord and the spiritual master, but we must know him as a manifestation of the Lord's mercy.

## 46

## What is the meaning of Śrī Guru?

The literal meaning of guru is "heavy." Why heavy? The original guru is Kṛṣṇa, and He is heavier than the Himalayan mountain range. He possesses immense gravity, for His task is to deliver the fallen souls from the clutches of *māyā*. All initiating gurus are only representatives of Kṛṣṇa. Kṛṣṇa is the bright light that dispels the darkness of *māyā*. *Gu* refers to darkness and *ru* refers to the light that dispels darkness. He who gives us the light of divine love, which will eradicate the darkness created by ignorance, is called guru.

## 47

## Can women become initiating gurus?

Our identity is that we are spirit souls. Due to our *karma* we get the body of a man or a woman. We are to use this body for the Lord's service and attain His eternal abode. Jāhnavā Mātā is an example of a Vaiṣṇavī guru. She is the potency of

Lord Nityānanda and Anaṅga Mañjarī in the spiritual abode. If a woman possesses qualifications such as Jāhnavā Mātā, then of course such a category of woman can become an initiating guru. Like any other guru, this would have to be approved and appointed by an *ācārya* in the line of disciplic succession to make it bona fide.

## 48
## Is the divine godliness of the spiritual master equivalent to that of the Supreme Lord?

The Supreme Lord Śrī Kṛṣṇa is incomparable; no one is greater than or equal to Him. Everybody is subordinate to Śrī Kṛṣṇa. The divine godliness of the spiritual master is equal to the extent that he is dear to the Supreme Lord. How dear one is to the Supreme Lord is based on how much the spiritual master chants the Hare Kṛṣṇa *mahā-mantra* with love and devotion in a pure state of consciousness. Śrīla Prabhupāda Bhaktisiddhānta Sarasvatī Ṭhākura repeatedly emphasized that the presence of one's Vaiṣṇava qualities is directly related to how much taste one has for the holy name (*yāra yata nāme ruci tāra tata vaiṣṇava ta*). A pure Vaiṣṇava is always extremely dear to Śrī Kṛṣṇa. This dearness to the Lord is the basis on which spiritual masters gain divine godliness, but they can never actually be equal to the Lord.

## 49

## Do the spiritual master and the members of the *guru-paramparā* only reside in the *maṭhas* and temples that they have established?

The spiritual master and all the members of the *guru-paramparā* are most dear to the Supreme Lord. Only he who is established in worshiping the Supreme Lord through pure devotional service can be dear to Him.

Suppose we do not follow our spiritual master's teachings. Perhaps we give up chanting the holy names in a humble state of mind and stop offering respect to one and all. Instead, we endeavor for material gain, worship, and position. We indulge our speculative independence and try to become the authority of a *maṭha* or temple, or we begin making allegations, politics, litigation, and engaging in verbal and physical fighting in order to gain authority over a center. Why would the spiritual master and members of the *guru-paramparā* want to stay in such a *maṭha* or temple, which has now turned into place of turmoil, agitation, and inquietude?

In reality, the spiritual master and the members of the *guru-paramparā* are the representatives of eternal peace, joy, bliss, and divine love. The Supreme Lord, Śrī Kṛṣṇa, is unparalleled and incomparable. The spiritual master and the other pure devotees of the *guru-paramparā* are the living form of Śrī Kṛṣṇa's mercy. Therefore they eternally reside by the side of those practicing pure, loving devotional service. People who practice pure devotion to the Supreme Lord never find faults in others and never get involved in fights, problems, litigation, etc. They stay away from all these agitating circumstances and instead stay in places conducive for the worship of Śrī Kṛṣṇa through pure devotional service.

If we would like for our spiritual master and the members of the *guru-paramparā* to stay in the *maṭhas* and temples, then we should constantly practice being humble and tolerant, give up the desire for material position and recognition, and offer due respect to all living entities. Along with developing these qualities, we should imbue the entire environment in the *maṭhas* and temples with the holy names. This is of the utmost importance. This type of behavior can keep the whole environment peaceful. Thus, Vaiṣṇavas possessing these qualities bring about a peaceful environment wherever they may be. Śrī Kṛṣṇa eternally resides in the hearts of such Vaiṣṇavas. The spiritual master and predecessor members of the *guru-paramparā* are present wherever Kṛṣṇa is present.

## 50
## What is the difference between a *maṭha* and a temple?

The main difference between a *maṭha* and a temple is that pure devotees live in a *maṭha* in order to exemplify and teach spiritual knowledge and practices regarding the ultimate goal of life. It can be said that a *maṭha* is a center for gaining transcendental knowledge (*paramārthika-śikṣā-kendra*). *Maṭhas* will generally have temples within their premises, and the presiding deities of the Supreme Lord are also present there. The presiding deity of the *maṭha* helps us to understand how to serve Him through the happiness of His pure devotees. In other words, the pure devotee will be satisfied when service to the deity is performed with love and great care. When the practices are not being performed properly, the pure devotee may feel the symptoms of the Lord's displeasure. The Supreme Lord even tastes the offerings that we give Him through the tongues of His pure devotees.

The main difference between a *maṭha* and a temple is that in those temples functioning without the guidance of the Lord's representative in the form of a pure devotee, the main deity remains silent. There He is served by the *brāhmaṇas,* who may not have an adequate understanding of the path of pure devotion. Worship of the Lord not endowed with pure devotion does not attract the attention of the Lord, and for that reason the Lord is not so inclined to accept the offerings of such *brāhmaṇas*. He remains silent to them, not revealing Himself or His full glory. Usually, pure devotees are not given facility to stay in these types of temples. Furthermore, there are usually no arrangements for obtaining spiritual knowledge about the ultimate goal of life.

## 51

## If a *maṭha* does not also contain a temple within its premises, can that institution still be called a *maṭha*?

The people who live in a *maṭha* stay there for the purpose of gaining spiritual knowledge regarding the ultimate goal of life. Their hearts gradually become free from unwanted motives and desires by chanting the holy names. When their hearts become completely free of these unwanted material motives and desires, then the Supreme Lord Himself manifests within their hearts. From then onward, the Supreme Lord constantly remains manifest in their hearts. Their hearts are transformed into temples of the Lord. Even if a temple is not externally present on the premises of the *maṭha,* each and every pure devotee's heart is a temple to the Supreme Lord. Thus, there are as many temples present in the *maṭha* as there are pure devotees living there.

## 52
## What is our shelter: the *maṭha,* the temple, or Śrī Kṛṣṇa's lotus feet?

Our actual shelter is the divine lotus feet of Śrī Kṛṣṇa. The pure devotees staying in the *maṭha* are living examples of how to take shelter of Śrī Kṛṣṇa's divine lotus feet. Therefore our initial shelter is the divine lotus feet of the pure devotees. By taking shelter of the pure devotees' lotus feet and by gaining their mercy, we will eventually be able to serve the eternal shelter—Śrī Kṛṣṇa's divine lotus feet.

## 53

## If there are no pure devotees living in a *maṭha*, can that place rightly be called a *maṭha* or an *āśrama*?

Pure devotees are the fundamental inspiration of establishing a *maṭha;* therefore each *maṭha* has a founding *ācārya*. Even if such an *ācārya* or pure devotee is not physically present there, their existence is always present in the *maṭha*. The residents of the *maṭha* should keep this understanding in mind and avoid arguments and creating a ruckus. They should establish the instructions of their spiritual master, the embodiment of pure devotion, in their hearts. They should not find faults in other Vaiṣṇavas and they should offer due respect to all the Vaiṣṇavas. Furthermore, they should chant the holy names with devotion from the core of their hearts. If the residents of the *maṭha* follow all of these principles, then even in the physical absence of a pure devotee, that institution can still be called a *maṭha* or *āśrama*.

But if we think, "Now that our spiritual master has left this world, let us start fighting over the property of this *maṭha*," or "We should convert the *maṭha* into a profitable business, and in such a way just make a show of chanting the holy names for the public," then that institution, which is lacking the principles of Vaiṣṇava behavior and etiquette, can no longer be called a *maṭha* or *āśrama*.

My spiritual master, Śrīla Bhakti Pramode Purī Gosvāmī Ṭhākura, frequently used to tell us that if we began to behave like this, then a poisonous cobra would be residing in the *maṭhas* and temples instead of the Supreme Lord. Instead of the practice of devotional service there would just be fighting and mayhem. How can institutions in which such a ruckus is taking place be called *maṭhas* or *āśramas*?

## 54
## What is the main purpose of a *maṭha* or *āśrama*?

The main purpose of a *maṭha* or *āśrama* is the deliverance of *jīvātmās* from the cycle of birth and death. It is a place for learning and practicing spiritual and religious duties (*ātmā-dharma*), as prescribed by the perfect authorities, so that one can reach the divine abode of the Supreme Lord. Moreover, through their own practice of the spiritual path, those souls residing in the *maṭha* serve as living examples to teach others how to obtain the ultimate goal of life and be delivered from the bondage of this material world.

55

Nowadays, the guru business appears prevalent. There are family gurus (*kula-gurus*), impersonalist gurus (*māyāvādī-gurus*), etc. People sometimes take shelter of these gurus. Later, they come in contact with a pure Vaiṣṇava guru and take shelter of that pure guru's lotus feet. Are these people implicated in the fault of giving up their guru (*guru-tyāga*) when they renounce their previous *kula-guru* or *māyāvādī-guru* and take shelter of a pure Vaiṣṇava guru?

First of all, we have to analyze if one's *kula-guru* is from an authorized *sampradāya* or if he is a so-called guru due to familial tradition despite not following any prescribed scriptural principles. For assessing the genuineness of a *kula-guru*, one must first see if he is coming from a Vaiṣṇava *sampradāya* that accepts Mahāprabhu. Then one must see if he follows the principles of *vaiṣṇava-dharma*. One can then assess if he is maintaining pure eating habits and other regulations, as well as practicing humility and tolerance, and whether or not he is bereft of desires for material gain and worship, or if he is greedy in any way. One should particularly note if he is genuinely attached to chanting the holy names daily, while offering due respect to everyone.

If the *kula-guru* fits all of the above-mentioned principles, then somebody who has already taken shelter at his lotus feet may be implicated in the offense of renouncing a bona fide guru (*guru-tyāga*) by leaving that *kula-guru* for the shelter of another pure Vaiṣṇava guru. However, if one is sheltered under a *māyāvādī-guru*, then that person can, on finding a Vaiṣṇava guru who is a pure devotee, immediately give up his shelter without hesitation. Of course, the Vaiṣṇava guru should be coming in an authorized line from Śrī Kṛṣṇa Caitanya Mahāprabhu, and he should be authorized to be guru by the previous members of the *sampradāya*. This pure devotee Vaiṣṇava guru should be practicing exemplary Vaiṣṇava behavior and etiquette. On taking shelter of such a spiritual master, Kṛṣṇa will become pleased from the core of His heart. Therefore there is no question of committing an offense by renouncing the previous guru.

The spiritual master is the embodiment of the mercy of Śrī Kṛṣṇa. He is the Supreme Lord in the role of a servant—*sevaka-bhagavān*. Through their practical example, the Vaiṣṇava spiritual masters teach those surrendered to their lotus feet how to serve Śrī Śrī Rādhā-Kṛṣṇa. If some *kula-guru,* instead of giving spiritual knowledge, seeks out disciples for financial gain, then giving up such a *kula-guru* for the shelter of a pure Vaiṣṇava will not implicate one in the *guru-tyāga* offense. The soul is the eternal servant of Kṛṣṇa; that is his eternal constitutional position. The servant always serves the master. Our eternal master is the Supreme Lord. The actual responsibility of the spiritual master is to reestablish souls in their eternal constitutional position by teaching them this knowledge of how to serve the Supreme Lord.

However, if a guru becomes greedy and decides that he will accept many, many disciples and give initiation to somebody who is already initiated by and sheltered under another pure Vaiṣṇava guru, then both the greedy guru and the disciple are implicated in offenses against devotees (*vaiṣṇava-aparādha*). This is why pure Vaiṣṇava gurus must be very careful before giving somebody initiation again.

## 56

## If a disciple loses faith in the spiritual master, can that disciple take shelter of another spiritual master within the same *sampradāya*? Will that disciple be at fault for giving up the previous spiritual master (*guru-tyāga*)?

In Sanskrit, a disciple is *śiṣyā*. *Śiṣyā* means one who has wholeheartedly accepted the discipline (*śāsana*) of the spiritual master. If the disciple acts in opposition to the instructions of the spiritual master and abandons his wishes, then the disciple has not accepted the discipline of the spiritual master. In such circumstances, *guru-tyāga* has already occurred and one has given up the spiritual master.

However, in very special cases of a highly qualified disciple, if one acts in opposition to the instructions of the spiritual master in order to please the spiritual master even more, then in that case, even though it may externally seem that the disciple has not accepted the discipline of the spiritual master, in reality that action of the disciple is accepted as service to the spiritual master (*guru-sevā*).

I hope that the readers are able to understand that *guru-tyāga,* or giving up the spiritual master, does not occur just by accepting *mantras* from another spiritual master. Rather, if one purposefully acts in opposition to the instructions of the spiritual master, if he does not fulfill the desires of the spiritual master and instead leads his life according to the demands and speculations of his own mind, then in such cases, the renunciation of his guru (*guru-tyāga*) has already taken place.

If a disciple makes a show of surrendering to a spiritual master while actually having some materialistic propensities and intentions in mind, then that disciple has not truly taken shelter of the Vaiṣṇava spiritual master. In the future, when that disciple's materialistic propensities are not fulfilled, that disciple will begin to find fault with the spiritual master. The show of apparent surrender to a spiritual master does not mean that the person has genuinely accepted the spiritual master. In this situation, if that spiritual master possesses all of the qualifications that a God-realized spiritual master (*sad-guru*) should possess—namely that he is free from offending devotees, does not desire to gratify his senses, and has not become an impersonalist (*māyāvādī*)—then the so-called disciple who has made a show of surrendering to this spiritual master gets implicated in the grave fault of offending a devotee (*vaiṣṇava-aparādha*).

Due to this offense, that person will never be able to take shelter of the lotus feet of another Vaiṣṇava. Even if that person apparently gets initiated into Vaiṣṇava *mantras* from someone else, the Supreme Lord will never accept any service from that individual due to the offense committed to a devotee. In this case, the so-called disciple, giving up all mundane desires for material gain, should completely and sincerely surrender to the first spiritual master and accept initiation into Vaiṣṇava *mantras* from the first spiritual master once again.

On the other hand, let us say that the first spiritual master does not possess the qualities of a genuine God-realized spiritual master (*sad-guru*), meaning that he offends devotees, desires to gratify his senses, or has become an impersonalist (*māyāvādī*). In this case, if the disciple rejects this spiritual master and takes shelter of the lotus feet of a God-realized Vaiṣṇava spiritual master, then the disciple is not at fault for rejecting his guru (*guru-tyāga*).

One does not become a spiritual master through pretense. This is why a disciple would not be at fault for rejecting the inauthentic spiritual master. In such a situation, we must understand that the Supreme Lord, becoming pleased with the previous virtuous deeds of the disciple, has bestowed His mercy on that spiritual aspirant through bringing the spiritual aspirant to the shelter of His true representative, the genuine spiritual master.

## 57
## Can an initiated disciple change his spiritual master by accepting initiation from another spiritual master?

One cannot change his or her initiating spiritual master. However, there are exceptions. Sometimes, a spiritual master is not actually authorized by the *guru-paramparā*. Although unauthorized, he may give discourses in such an enchanting manner that the listeners accept him as their spiritual master. At other times, a spiritual master promotes himself to that position, thinking himself qualified, although he is neither appointed nor authorized. Sometimes, a meeting is held and somebody is voted to become a spiritual master when he does not actually meet the qualifications. In such situations, changing one's initiating spiritual master is acceptable and not a fault.

Furthermore, a disciple can change his or her spiritual master under the following circumstances:

(1) The spiritual master gives up *vaiṣṇava-dharma* and/or becomes a *māyāvādī* (impersonalist).

(2) The spiritual master becomes greedy for money.

(3) The spiritual master begins criticizing other Vaiṣṇavas and engaging in offenses against the Vaiṣṇavas.

(4) The spiritual master becomes desirous of satisfying his senses and engages in illicit relationships.

Changing one's spiritual master by taking shelter of another spiritual master is not subject to fault in the aforementioned circumstances.

❖❖❖

## 58

## We have read the following quotes from the *Mantra-muktāvalī,* which are quoted by Gopāla Bhaṭṭa Gosvāmī and Sanātana Gosvāmī in the *Hari-bhakti-vilāsa* (1.38–40), the rulebook for all Gauḍīya Vaiṣṇavas:

*avadātānvayaḥ śuddhaḥ svocitācāra-tat-paraḥ*
*āśramī krodha-rahito vedavit sarva-śāstravit*

*śraddhāvān anasūyaś ca priya-vāk priya-darśanaḥ*
*śuciḥ suveṣas taruṇaḥ sarva-bhūta-hite rataḥ*
*dhīmān anuddhata-matiḥ pūrṇo 'hantā vimarśakaḥ*
*sad-guṇo 'rcāsu kṛtadhīḥ kṛtajñaḥ śiṣya-vatsalaḥ*

These are the prescribed qualifications that one must possess in order to serve as an initiating spiritual master. In this verse, the word *avadātānvayaḥ* is used, which means that the initiating spiritual master must be born in a pure, spotless family lineage. What exactly does that mean?

Purity of birth is determined by the Vedic scriptures. They state that the mother must have been chaste at the time of conception of the child who will grow up to become a spiritual master. According to the revealed scriptures, every single living entity has the right to engage in *hari-bhajana* (worship of the Lord). However, there are many rules and laws in the revealed scriptures regarding one taking up the role of *dīkṣā-guru* and engaging others in *hari-bhajana*. According to the opinion of the revealed scriptures, one must have taken birth in the approved Vedic manner in order to be qualified to take up the role of an initiating spiritual master.

Furthermore, we must understand that the actual seed-giving father is the Supreme Lord, Śrī Kṛṣṇa. Here, the father gives the seed and the mother is like the earth. The seed, which is originally given by the Supreme Lord, is always pure. However, if the earth is not fertile, then the living entity born from that seed cultivated in the infertile soil will never grow into a healthy child ornamented with transcendental qualities. If the living entity is not sufficiently nourished by the earth (just as it is not nourished when in the seed-like form), then the child born of such an unchaste mother's womb, according to the revealed Vedic scriptures, can never attain the transcendental qualities needed to serve as an initiating spiritual master. However, in this matter, if the father was involved in intimate relationships before marriage, where he lost his virginity, but the mother has always been chaste, then the child born from this couple's union is most definitely qualified to take up the role of an initiating spiritual master, given that he is anointed with all the other qualities needed for serving as such.

A potential initiating spiritual master must be free of material false ego, having himself taken shelter at the lotus feet of a genuine spiritual master. Furthermore, he must be free of committing offenses (i.e. free from the ten offenses against the holy names, the ten offenses against the holy *dhāma,* and the thirty-two offenses in rendering service to the deity of the Lord) and should unfailingly engage in chanting the *mahā-mantra* of the Lord with love and devotion every day. All of the above-mentioned qualities must be present in a person for him to be considered qualified to serve as an initiating spiritual master. For this reason, it is not that the only disqualification for becoming an initiating spiritual master is to have been born from a mother who was unchaste at the time of conception. If the other qualities mentioned above are not comprehensively present in a devotee, then he can never take up the position of an initiating spiritual master.

For example, Rāvaṇa's mother was a demon princess known as Kaikaśi; his father was a *brāhmaṇa* sage known as Viśravā. As we can see, although the father was a great sage, his children turned out to be demons—Rāvaṇa and Kumbhakarṇa. Another example is Prahlāda Mahārāja. Prahlāda's mother was a pious lady known as Kayādhu; his father was a demon known as Hiraṇyakaśipu. As we know, Prahlāda turned out to be a great devotee.

## 59
## Why do people worship guru similar to the way they worship God?

Due to our unwanted mundane desires we are not eligible to get Kṛṣṇa's mercy directly. Since Kṛṣṇa is very merciful and wants us to attain Him, He sends His representatives (Śrī Guru) to us. Kṛṣṇa's mercy is appearing to us in the condensed form of Śrī Guru. Therefore we worship guru as God's expansion of mercy.

## 60
## How do we receive guru's mercy?

In Sanskrit, mercy is called *kṛpa*. Whatever happens to be the guru's desire for our spiritual progress, according to his guidance we should follow his instructions and thereby become recipients of his mercy. The inner meaning of the word *kṛpa* implies that our activities are favorable to the object of our service, which in this case are activities that please the guru.

## 61
## Can an initiating guru ever reject his disciples?

The connection between the guru and the disciple is eternal. A bona fide guru will never reject his disciples. The spiritual master is not an individual. He is *tattva* (truth), *akhaṇḍa-guru-tattva*. This means that the principle of guru is one, and in actuality the spiritual master is the entire *paramparā*, for he is the embodiment of all the previous gurus. As explained earlier, gurus are the mercy expansions of the Supreme Lord and are therefore extremely merciful, so how could they reject their disciples?

# III

# Vaishnava Dharma and Sadhana

## 62
## What is *dharma*?

Śrīla Prabhupāda Bhaktisiddhānta Sarasvatī Gosvāmī Ṭhākura said in one discourse that the *jīvātmā's* eternal constitutional nature is its eternal *dharma*. If we engage in philosophical exploration to seek out the eternal nature of the soul, then we can see that every embodied soul desires eternal happiness, peace, love, and bliss, which is, in reality, the Supreme Lord, Śrī Kṛṣṇa. This Kali-yuga is filled with quarrel, hypocrisy, deceit, and crookedness. The path to attain Śrī Kṛṣṇa in this age is to take shelter of and receive initiation from a pure devotee spiritual master who is authorized by the entire *guru-paramparā*. Then by chanting the holy names with love and devotion, without offenses, we can attain the Supreme Lord Śrī Kṛṣṇa and taste that eternal happiness, peace, love, and bliss for which we have all been hankering. All spiritual authorities and Vedic scriptures explain that the *dharma* of Kali-yuga is to chant the holy names.

## 63
## What is *ātmā-dharma*? How can we nourish the soul?

Each living entity is a soul (*ātmā*). *Dharma* is the eternal, natural function of the soul. The real function of the soul is to be eternally blissful and peaceful. *Ātmā-dharma* means to feed the soul. Out of ignorance we may think that whatever food we eat is food for the soul, but actually it is not. Instead, we are feeding the body and starving our real selves, the soul. In actuality, all that food is material food meant for nourishing the material body. We can see that we may be physically fit, but we are not genuinely happy at all. Whatever temporary happiness we may be feeling is just a reflection of the eternal happiness of the soul. Such temporary happiness is not real happiness at all. This is because the soul is hungry and is crying for nourishment.

The soul is moving through different bodies in the material cycle of birth and death. As soon as the soul attains a human body, it has the opportunity to practice different faiths. When we come to know from the revealed scriptures about the prescribed spiritual practice for this present age, we can begin to feed the soul and be on our way to eternal happiness. In this present age of quarrel (Kali-yuga), the scriptures prescribe that everyone chant the Lord's names. By such chanting the soul can easily be fed. Thus, by engaging in chanting for the satisfaction of the Supreme Lord Śrī Kṛṣṇa, the source of all souls, we will be able to be properly engaged in *ātmā-dharma*.

We feed our ears by listening to melodious music. We feed our tongues by tasting delicious foods, and so on. However, we fail to feed ourselves, the soul, our real identity. The soul is transcendental, a tiny fire spark coming from the supersoul, which is the embodiment of the Supreme Lord, Śrī Kṛṣṇa. Śrī Kṛṣṇa appeared in the age of quarrel in this material world as the Hare Kṛṣṇa *mahā-mantra*. The holy name is coming from the transcendental abode. That holy name is transcendental food for the soul. When we faithfully engage in chanting the holy name, the Hare Kṛṣṇa *mahā-mantra*, then we are feeding the soul. Thus, we will eventually attain our *ātmā-dharma* and be eternally blissful and peaceful.

## 64
## What are the important qualities and etiquette in *vaiṣṇava-dharma*?

It is of the utmost importance that the followers of *vaiṣṇava-dharma* are humble, tolerant, and free from even a drop of desire for material gain, worship, and status. Followers of this *dharma* must offer appropriate respect to all *jīvas* and systematically chant the Hare Kṛṣṇa *mahā-mantra* daily with love. In this way, success will be achieved.

## 65
## Rather than taking shelter of a spiritual master, if we buy chanting beads from the market and chant the *mahā-mantra*, will this not give Śrī Kṛṣṇa happiness?

If we chant the Hare Kṛṣṇa *mahā-mantra*, then we are undoubtedly benefited. However, if we buy chanting beads from the market and chant on them without taking shelter of the spiritual master, we will only gain the benefit of having our sins washed away and gaining pious credits (*puṇya*). These pious credits can only give us material facilities and temporary material happiness; they will never allow the *jīva* to realize its constitutional identity as the eternal loving servant of Śrī Kṛṣṇa. Without realization of one's eternal spiritual identity, it is impossible to achieve divine love (*prema*).

The spiritual master, who should be a pure devotee, assesses the surrender of the *jīva* and plants the seed of *kṛṣṇa-prema* (divine love of God) in the heart of an eligible recipient. If we surrender to the representative of Śrī Kṛṣṇa, the pure devotee, and go to him daily to hear and chant the glories (*hari-kathā*) and names of Hari (*hari-kīrtana*), then this hearing and chanting acts as the water to cultivate that seed of *kṛṣṇa-prema* that has been planted in the heart. Gradually, the seed of divine love will sprout and grow, and eventually the *jīva* becomes established in its eternal spiritual identity beyond this material world, to the transcendental spiritual realm of Goloka Vṛndāvana. The father of all *jīvas* is Śrī Kṛṣṇa. If the *jīva* becomes purified and goes to the father, then the father naturally becomes very pleased. By surrendering to the lotus feet of the pure devotee, who is accepted and appointed by the *paramparā*, and by daily chanting on *tulasī* beads given by the appointed spiritual master, the *jīvas* can give great happiness to Śrī Kṛṣṇa.

## 66

## Is it better to chant *harināma* on *tulasī* beads or on the small counter devices that have become popular in recent times?

The previous *ācāryas* have instructed us to chant the Hare Kṛṣṇa *mahā-mantra* at every single moment. Nowadays, there are some places and situations in society where people criticize, out of ignorance, those chanting on *tulasī* beads. This causes such critics to become victims of *aparādha* (offense). To ensure that such people don't fall into the deep ditch of offenses, and so that we also follow the instructions of the previous *ācāryas*, namely to chant the Hare Kṛṣṇa *mahā-mantra* at every single moment, it is acceptable to chant using the counter machines in such extreme situations. Nevertheless, it is important to remember that to provide the greatest pleasure to Lord Kṛṣṇa it is much better to chant on the *tulasī* beads given by the spiritual master.

## 67

## What are *anarthas* (unwanted spiritual impediments)?

There are four categories of *anarthas*, and each of these has four further divisions:

(1) *Svarūpa-bhrama:* to suffer any illusions regarding the nature of ultimate spiritual identity
   - (a) *Sva-tattva-bhrama* (or *jīva-svarūpa-bhrama*): illusion about one's own original identity
   - (b) *Paratattva-bhrama:* illusion about the spiritual identity of Bhagavān
   - (c) *Sādhya-sādhana-tattva-bhrama:* illusion regarding the *sādhya*, the ultimate

objective of spiritual attainment, which is *prema-bhakti;* and illusion regarding *sādhana-bhakti,* the means to attain *prema-bhakti*

(d) *Māyā-tattva-bhrama:* illusion regarding the Lord's *māyā,* or His external illusory energy

(2) *Asat-tṛṣṇā:* to thirst for the temporary—material enjoyment

(a) to thirst for material enjoyment in this world

(b) to thirst for enjoyment in the higher planetary systems, or heavenly planets

(c) to thirst after the eight mystic *siddhis* (powers)

(d) to thirst after impersonal liberation.

(3) *Aparādha:* offenses

(a) offenses toward Śrī Kṛṣṇa

(b) offenses toward *kṛṣṇa-nāma*

(c) offenses toward *kṛṣṇa-svarūpa* (the deity form of the Lord)

(d) offenses toward other *jīvas*

(4) *Hṛdaya-daurbalya:* weakness of heart

(a) *tuccha-āsakti:* attachment for useless things

(b) *kuṭināṭī:* deceitful behavior. The word

*kuṭināṭī* consists of *ku* ("bad" or "evil") and *na* or *nāṭi* ("that which is forbidden"). It means to perform any forbidden act.

(c) *mātsarya:* envy

(d) *sva-pratiṣṭhā-lālasā:* desire for fame, status, and adoration.

## 68

## Will we continue to have unfavorable tendencies even after taking shelter of the lotus feet of a genuine spiritual master (*sad-guru*)?

First, we must clearly understand the meaning of the word, *śiṣyā*. The word *śiṣyā* means one who genuinely accepts and follows the rules and regulations given by the spiritual master. A genuine spiritual master is one who has attained Śrī Kṛṣṇa. That is why the genuine spiritual master's tongue is always dancing with the pure chanting of the Hare Kṛṣṇa *mahā-mantra*. The genuine spiritual master always speaks about the glories of Śrī Kṛṣṇa as they are explained in the revealed scriptures and keeps himself far away from materialistic tendencies at all times. Being under the shelter of such a spiritual master and with our best effort to follow his instructions and guidance, we will gradually lose all unfavorable tendencies and pure devotional practices will appear in our hearts.

## 69

## Can a person who is chanting the *mahā-mantra* under the shelter of a bona fide guru still gain entry into Goloka Vṛndāvana if he is criticizing others?

Śrīla Vṛndāvana Dāsa Ṭhākura has written in *Śrī Caitanya Bhāgavata:*

*kāhāre na kare nindā, 'kṛṣṇa kṛṣṇa' bale*
*ajaya caitanya sei jinibeka hele*

"Do not criticize others but instead always chant the names of Kṛṣṇa! Kṛṣṇa! By this you will be able to conquer the unconquerable [Śrī Kṛṣṇa, or Śrī Caitanya]. In other words, you will win Them over."

Nanda-nandana Kṛṣṇa is filled with generosity

,and Śrīmatī Rādhārāṇī is filled with mercy. Śrī Kṛṣṇa Caitanya descended to earth decorated with the divine mood and complexion of Śrīmatī Rādhārāṇī. We can realize the teachings that Śrī Kṛṣṇa Caitanya Mahāprabhu practiced and preached only when we are completely free from the tendency to criticize others. We have to reach such a stage at which we are not even inclined to listen to somebody criticizing a third person. Not only that, but we have to wholeheartedly, very politely, imbued with sweet Vaiṣṇava qualities, request the criticizer to not engage in criticism. However, if the criticizer does not listen to our words, then we must immediately leave that place, saying, "Kṛṣṇa! Kṛṣṇa!"

Despite being sheltered under a genuine spiritual master and chanting the holy names, if we still find ourselves caught up in the tendency to speak and hear criticism, then we will never obtain the opportunity to enter into the Lord's eternal pastimes in Goloka Vṛndāvana.

Jagadānanda Paṇḍita has written in his book *Prema-vivarta* that even if such a critic chants the *mahā-mantra* for ten million births, that person will never be able to obtain service to the divine lotus feet of Śrī Kṛṣṇa.

We should all gradually give up this negative tendency to criticize others. By staying under the shelter of a genuine spiritual master, this tendency to criticize and find faults will be overcome in a very short time. We should practice our chanting of the *mahā-mantra* in a hopeful spirit. Kṛṣṇa is an ocean of mercy, and He will remove our fault-finding tendency from its very root.

❖❖❖

## 70
## Is it considered service toward our spiritual master if we try to expand the preaching of his institution by criticizing other Vaiṣṇava organizations?

It is said:

> *"kṛṣṇa rakṣati jagat trayam"—"guru"*

> Kṛṣṇa is the universal guru and He is the one who will protect and deliver us.

Śrī Kṛṣṇa Himself is the spiritual master of everyone. Other Vaiṣṇava organizations also worship Śrī Kṛṣṇa. Therefore if one criticizes other Vaiṣṇava organizations in order to expand the preaching of one's own initiating or instructing spiritual masters' organization, then how will Śrī Kṛṣṇa be pleased? Thus, this tendency to criticize simply causes one to engage in offenses against devotees (*vaiṣṇava-aparādha*). So rather than giving pleasure to the spiritual master one will earn his displeasure instead.

## 71

## If a guru instructs a disciple to criticize others or engage in non-devotional activities, then does the disciple become liable for committing those offenses?

The disciple is most definitely liable and is at fault for committing offenses. Not only the disciple, but the guru also becomes liable for the offenses committed. That said, a bona fide spiritual master never engages the disciple in any condemnable or non-devotional activities or tendencies. The guru thinks, "I may get cheated myself, but I will never cheat somebody else." The Vaiṣṇava spiritual master lives by this principle.

## 72
## Does a true Vaiṣṇava seek revenge when slighted?

The tendency to take revenge actually destroys a human being. If one has a tendency to take revenge, then that person begins to hate and hurt others and thinks of others as inferior. These qualities are all unfavorable to the path of becoming a true Vaiṣṇava. If such unfavorable qualities become established in the heart, they will cause one to fall into the lower species of life. Therefore a true Vaiṣṇava is free of the tendency to seek revenge. A genuine Vaiṣṇava is a true well-wisher of each and every living entity.

## 73
## Can true Vaiṣṇavas engage in positive debate?

They surely can. Their protest is done in a very gentlemanly manner, without any aggression. Pure Vaiṣṇavas can engage in debate to defend and/or establish a conclusion, as it is revealed in the scriptures, for the benefit of society. Pure Vaiṣṇavas appear for the sole purpose of bestowing auspiciousness upon all living entities. Those who are fortunate will know these Vaiṣṇavas as abodes of auspiciousness and will be able to recognize that their arguments are meant for the spiritual upliftment of society at large. Therefore it is fitting that each and every person in society offer appropriate respect to all pure Vaiṣṇavas, knowing them as the Supreme Lord's representatives. Such behavior is very pleasing to the Supreme Lord.

## 74
## Will our spiritual master deliver us even if we are not chanting the daily number

## of prescribed rounds, thinking that our service towards his society will compensate for our shortcomings in chanting?

The spiritual master connects us to the *guru-paramparā*. The instruction of the entire *guru-paramparā* is to (1) chant at least one hundred thousand holy names per day (sixty-four rounds) on one's *japa-mālā* (chanting beads) with utmost love and devotion, and (2) serve the Vaiṣṇavas.

Usually, due to our previous conditioning and activities, we are unable to follow these two instructions of the *guru-paramparā*. We must build a temple of devotion for the holy names in our heart and make our sole purpose to serve the Vaiṣṇavas. Due to not following the above instructions of the *guru-paramparā*, we end up constructing buildings and temples simply to fulfill our own material desire for position. We make hotels and places for guests to stay and engage in selling *prasādam*. Like this, we engage ourselves in so many nonessential activities and then say that we do not have enough time to chant the holy names.

If we do not develop a taste to chant the holy name and to hear about the Supreme Lord from the auspicious lips of pure devotees, then we will not have any taste to serve the Vaiṣṇavas. If somebody is hungry and if another person eats, then will the hungry person's stomach become full? No. If I am hungry, then I must eat. In the same way, if I do not chant the *mahā-mantra* sufficiently, then how can the spiritual master deliver me from this material world and take me to the spiritual world? I myself must chant the *mahā-mantra* with love and devotion and serve the devotees in order to purify my heart and rid it of all the unwanted desires and motives that pollute it.

If one desires to enjoy the senses on the pretext of devotion, then that person can never get the mercy of the spiritual master. Actually, the real mercy of the spiritual master is to show us the insignificance of finding pleasure in this material world of birth and death. Trying to find pleasure in the material world is born from material attachment. These material attachments force us back into the material world again and again and will never give us access to the spiritual world of Śrī Kṛṣṇa. The soul's true role is to establish its existence in the blissful spiritual world of Śrī Kṛṣṇa, and the method to attain this in Kali-yuga is to chant the *mahā-mantra*.

## 75

## In order to follow the practice of loving devotion (*vaiṣṇava-dharma*), it is necessary to serve the spiritual master. Is disliking other devotees in the name of serving one's own spiritual master a sign of devotion?

Never. Śrīla Bhaktivinoda Ṭhākura has said, *vaiṣṇava vidveṣa kari, chāḍe nāma rasa / krame krame haya artha kamanira basa:* "If one hates other devotees, then one's taste to chant the holy names is destroyed." Gradually, such persons will desire to collect more and more wealth and gratify their senses. Men will search for women in order to enjoy their senses, and women will be engaged in associating with men in uncivilized ways. This will never give rise to genuine service to the spiritual master.

## 76
## Is *manavatā* (possessing human qualities) the same as *vaiṣṇavatā* (possessing Vaiṣṇava qualities)?

Only the soul that possesses a human body can develop into a Vaiṣṇava. However, by the will of the Supreme Lord, the human form has no overriding instinctual nature. Rather, He has given these souls intelligence and independence. People will develop their natures based on the influence of the association that they take in this material world. The association that humans have from the time of their birth will influence them, and they will develop a particular nature. If they change their association, then their nature can be changed again.

Śrīla Kṛṣṇadāsa Kavirāja Gosvāmī has shown us how to develop a devotional nature centered on Śrī Kṛṣṇa in his *Śrī Caitanya-caritāmṛta: kṛṣṇa-bhakti-janma-mula haya sādhu-saṅga,* "Association with saintly devotees is the root cause of devotion to Śrī Kṛṣṇa." In this Kali-yuga, where people neglect to search after the Supreme Absolute Truth, there is an absence of saintly people. Consequently, we do not have such ample opportunity to associate with them. Thus we disregard any consideration of the scriptural understanding of *manavatā* and *vaiṣṇavatā* and instead act according to the impulses of our own mind.

Therefore *manavatā* and *vaiṣṇavatā* are described based on the association that people take. However, if we research the terms *manavatā* and *vaiṣṇavatā* in the revealed scriptures, it will be very difficult to find any difference between the two. Brahmā's son Manu was a natural Vaiṣṇava. We are called humans (*manuṣyā*) based on being descendants from Manu. Manu has composed a law book for mankind called the *Manu-Saṁhitā*. Therein, Manu has described five laws that are essential in order for one to be considered human. If one does not follow these five laws, then that person is considered to be a two-legged animal. The five laws of Manu are briefly described below:

*ahiṁsā satyamāsteyam śaucaṁ sāmyamameva ca*
*etat samasikam proktaṁ dharmasya pañca-lakṣaṇaṁ*
*(Manu-Saṁhitā)*

(1) Do not steal (*acauryam*):
The entire world is the property of Kṛṣṇa, yet we must take things from this world to maintain our lives. Kṛṣṇa provides many types of eatables so that we may nourish our bodies. Thus, according

to Vaiṣṇava principles, we should offer whatever we eat first to the Lord. We should never eat anything that the Lord does not accept. The Lord instructs us to offer Him leaves, flowers, fruits, water, milk, etc. Following this instruction of the Lord, Vaiṣṇavas offer these products to the Lord before honoring them as *prasādam,* and in this way they do not get the reaction of stealing. Taking things from others without asking them is theft. By offering the Supreme Lord's property to Him, we are not stealing. Thus, following this principle, if everything is used for the Lord's service, one is properly situated.

(2) Leading one's life according to the revealed scriptures (*sāmyam*):
Manu says that human beings should lead their lives according to the revealed scriptures. Humans should not lead their lives according to their mind's whimsical desires, and they should definitely not scare others into submission by intimidating them through their physical and financial prowess. By neglecting the rule of *sāmyam,* society gets entangled in theft, illicit connection with the opposite sex, robbery, murder, and the desire

for material gain and position. In this way, people do not follow the revealed scriptures and this rule of *sāmyam* is violated.

The scriptures conclude that the Supreme Lord is the one and only controller and maintainer of the world. If we become surrendered to Śrī Kṛṣṇa, then we will become humble and tolerant. The desire for material gain, worship, position, and the weaknesses of enviousness and a political mindset are the source of unrest in society. These tendencies, at their very root, are easily driven away by surrendering to the Supreme Lord and His authorized representative. Furthermore, we must offer appropriate respect to everyone in society and maintain a peaceful atmosphere. This is the meaning of the word *sāmyam*. Vaiṣṇavas perfectly follow these characteristics of a *manavatā* and thereby give happiness to the Supreme Lord through their perfect conduct.

(3) Nonviolence (*ahiṁsā*):
The Supreme Lord created the world in such a way that one living entity maintains its life by eating another. For example, cows eat grass, whereas carnivores such as tigers and lions, eat the cows. Tiny

bugs eat the tender grass, and the frogs in turn eat those tiny insects. Snakes eat the frogs, peacocks eat the snakes, while other predatory animals in turn eat the peacocks when they are given the slightest opportunity to do so.

Despite this natural behavior of animals, human beings are competent to lead nonviolent lives. This is why the Supreme Lord has given the human beings a way to be protected from the sin of killing other living entities: that is, by first offering acceptable food to the Supreme Lord. The Supreme Lord only accepts *sattvic* preparations, such as those made from leaves, flowers, fruits, and milk. Even though these foods are still living entities, Kṛṣṇa says that by offering them to Him with love and devotion, He will liberate those living entities. Kṛṣṇa further explains that when the food items are honored after being offered to Him as a means to maintain one's life, then the human being will not incur any sin. Maintaining one's life in this way will not be an obstacle in following Manu's law of nonviolence.

(4) Cleanliness (*suddhata*):
We may all display cleanliness externally, but genuine cleanliness refers to the purity of heart and

mind. The dirt of the heart and mind cannot be cleaned by any material object or means. This dirt can only be cleaned through the association of genuine seekers of the Absolute Truth and by chanting the Hare Kṛṣṇa *mahā-mantra* while remaining aloof from offenses. Those who chant the holy names are known as Vaiṣṇavas.

(5) Truthfulness (*satya*):
We cannot take shelter of the eternal truth simply by speaking truthful words in the course of our mundane daily discussions. The actual eternal truth is the Supreme Lord Śrī Kṛṣṇa. Taking shelter of Him and leading one's life according to His teachings is of the utmost need in society. In this Kali-yuga, the method to take shelter of the Supreme Lord Śrī Kṛṣṇa is to chant the Hare Kṛṣṇa *mahā-mantra* without committing offenses. The rule of truthfulness, which is a part of *manavatā*, is inherent in the concept of *vaiṣṇavatā*.

Through logical analysis one can see that the principle of *manavatā* and *vaiṣṇavatā* is non-different, and that the Vaiṣṇava's behavior is the fulfillment of Manu's laws.

## 77
## Does solitary worship (*nirjana-bhajana*) mean to sit in one place all alone and chant the *mahā-mantra*?

First of all, the word *bhajana* means to serve the Supreme Lord and everything related to the Lord. To serve means to please through our actions. Śrī Nayana-maṇi Mañjarī is one of the dearest personal associates of Śrīmatī Rādhārāṇī (Kṛṣṇa's bliss-bestowing potency). The Gauḍīya Maṭha and various movements under its banner, including ISKCON, recognize Nayana-maṇi Mañjarī as having descended as Śrīla Prabhupāda Bhaktisiddhānta Sarasvatī Gosvāmī Ṭhākura in this Kali-yuga. Śrīla Prabhupāda has written the following verse in one of his *kīrtanas:*

*duṣṭa mana! tumi kisera vaiṣṇava?*
*pratiṣṭhāra tare, nirjanera ghare,*
*tava harināma kevala kaitava*

O evil mind! What type of Vaiṣṇava are you? You sit in solitude making a show of engaging in chanting the holy names. You

> are doing this just to be recognized as a great person by society. Your chanting of the holy names is totally hypocritical. (*Vaiṣṇava Ke?,* Verse 1)

If we engage in solitary worship with a desire to be recognized by society as a greatly elevated *bhajanānandī* (one who is engaged in secluded worship), then our chanting of the holy names is merely a deception. Chanting the *mahā-mantra* in solitude with such a mindset is utter hypocrisy. *Kaitava,* or hypocrisy, means that one's words and actions are inconsistent with each other. Such hypocrisy violates *vaiṣṇava-dharma*. Yet we also must refer to anyone who chants the *mahā-mantra* as Vaiṣṇavas. Śrīla Prabhupāda has described that the desire for worldly recognition is like hog's stool. Chanting the *mahā-mantra* in solitude, with a mind possessed of such evil intelligence, is nothing but hypocrisy.

## 78

## Can we please the Supreme Lord by singing beautiful *kīrtana* melodies and dancing in an enchanting and intoxicating style?

The Supreme Lord, Śrī Kṛṣṇa, is pleased solely by a devotee's sincerity and loving devotional service. The ultimate goal of *bhakti,* or devotional service, is to please Śrī Kṛṣṇa. The goal is not to impress people of this world with melodious and intoxicating *kīrtana,* music, or dance. Nobody can see our heart except for the Supreme Lord, so we should not try to deceive Him. If we sing *kīrtana* melodiously and dance enchantingly in the name of service to the Supreme Lord, while we are actually doing such activities just to show off to society and gain recognition, then in reality we are merely engaging in deceit and hypocrisy. We will never be able to please the Supreme Lord in this way. Śrīla Prabhupāda has written in one of his *kīrtanas:*

*śrīdayitadāsa, kīrtanate āśa,*
*kara uccaī svare 'harināma-rava*
*kīrtana-prabhāve, smaraṇa svabhāve,*
*se kāle bhajana-nirjana sambhava*
(*Vaiṣṇava Ke?,* Verse 19)

The word *smaraṇa* means to remember the Supreme Lord's divine pastimes. By loudly chanting and singing the holy names (*uccaḥsvare-kīrtana*), we will eventually become free of unwanted motives and desires (*anarthas*) and will then be able to remember the divine pastimes of the Supreme Lord. Śrīla Prabhupāda has explained that to be free of unwanted motives and desires means to not want material gain, worship, or position. The Supreme Lord will be pleased with our *kīrtana* and worship when our worship is for His pleasure only and we desire nothing for ourselves.

## 79
## Can we be clever in dealing with the Supreme Lord?

Śrī Kṛṣṇa is the crown jewel of all clever people. Our true identity in cleverness and intelligence will manifest when we engage in serving devotees and chant the *mahā-mantra* with the hope of attaining service to Śrī Kṛṣṇa's divine lotus feet. Serving devotees actually means to serve the pure and unalloyed devotees of Śrī Kṛṣṇa. By serving such pure devotees, one will receive their blessings and be more inclined and serious on the path of devotional service. Such blessings will help us to chant the holy names in a pure way. Chanting the *mahā-mantra* purely has the strength to attract Śrī Kṛṣṇa. He will descend from His supreme abode of Goloka Vṛndāvana in order to be within the proximity of His pure devotee. Śrīla Bhaktivinoda Ṭhākura has written in one of his *kīrtanas:*

*śuddha-bhakata-caraṇa-reṇu, bhajana-anukūla*
*bhakata-sevā, parama-siddhi, prema-latikāra mūla*
(*Śuddha Bhakata,* Verse 1)

Actual intelligence and cleverness is to engage in the devotional service of Śrī Kṛṣṇa following the two abovementioned paths, namely serving pure devotees and purely chanting the holy names. This type of intelligence is proper when dealing with the Supreme Lord. However, engaging in fashionable dance and music in the name of devotional service is often seen nowadays, such as some of the professional, week-long *bhāgavat-saptāhas* and Bengali village *pala-kīrtanas.* The performers in these programs follow absolutely no rules and regulations as far as *vaiṣṇava-dharma* is concerned. Such people are simply trying to gratify their senses and make a profitable business from their religious activities. This type of "cleverness," which is a misuse of one's intelligence and makes a show of religion as a means to make money, is never authorized when dealing with the Supreme Lord.

## 80

## If we go to the temple to offer worship to the Lord, but in our heart we cherish the desire to fulfill our own goals and material desires, are we practicing *dharma*?

Happiness derived from the fulfillment of material desires is like an itching disease. In the first stage of the itching disease, the sick person scratches the place where he or she feels the itch, feeling immense relief. But just as the person stops scratching, he or she feels an intense burning sensation. Thus, if we analyze this according to the actual definition of *dharma*, we realize that *dharma* is not being followed at all by worshiping the Lord for the fulfillment of one's material desires. Material desires make us feel like we are going to achieve immense happiness, but then they throw us again into the ocean of material suffering, just like one suffering from an itching disease. The actual meaning of *dharma* is to obtain the Supreme Lord, who is the form of eternal bliss. By obtaining the Lord, we obtain everything our heart desires. We will never have anything lacking and will be supremely happy.

## 81

## Is there hope for one to advance spiritually even though the circumstances surrounding one's birth may be dubious?

All souls have one inherent qualification: their connection to the Supreme Lord, which thereby gives them the eligibility to worship Him. It is of the ultimate benefit for all to engage in the prescribed worship of the Supreme Lord according to the age (*yuga*) one is living in. In Satya-yuga the process was meditation (*dhyāna*); in Tretā-yuga the process was to engage in fire sacrifices (*yajña*); in Dvāpara-yuga the process was to engage in worshiping the deity (*pūjā*); and in this Kali-yuga the process is to chant the names of the Supreme Lord while eating, sleeping, and in all circumstances at every single moment of time. This is the prescription of the revealed scriptures. This is why in this Kali-yuga, everybody, regardless of caste, creed, occupation, etc., must engage in chanting the holy names of the Supreme Lord. Those who are truly intelligent engage in appropriate activities that will allow them to be eternally liberated from the suffering and sadness of this material world. Thus, regardless of the circumstances of one's birth, it is the duty of every single embodied soul to vow to serve the Supreme Lord in all circumstances, through every single action. One should especially become devoted to the chanting of the Hare Kṛṣṇa *mahā-mantra,* which is the source of all perfection in the current age.

## 82
## Do we obtain a specific birth due to the fruits of our previous actions?

Most certainly. People obtain a particular body due to the fruits of their previous actions. Even if we get human bodies, we will take birth in a family most suited for us to enjoy and suffer the results of our previous actions. We get a birth in a rich and materially wealthy family due to past piety. According to our sinful activities, we will take birth in circumstances that are best suited for suffering the results of those sins. If we are particularly pious, or sincerely dedicated to the Supreme Lord, we may even be born in a family of devotees. In this way, one can have an ideal start to practice the path of *bhāgavata-dharma* and associate with devotees from the very beginning of one's life. In this Kali-yuga however, no matter what birth, everyone should endeavor to make his or her life perfect by cultivating devotion to the Supreme Lord.

## 83
## Who is fortunate?

The soul that is inclined to practice the path of devotion is most fortunate. Individuals who are materially minded will consider those having material wealth and comfort as being most fortunate. However, the revealed scriptures state that those who are very desirous of material sense enjoyment are most unfortunate. Material sense objects only have the ability to give some meager temporary happiness. Those who are fortunate will see past such endeavors for temporary happiness, instead looking toward the eternal happiness of the soul in its relation with the Supreme Lord.

## 84
## What is meant by spirituality (*paramārtha*)?

*Artha* means actions that provide material gain; and *paramārtha* means actions that provide spiritual gain. Previously we established the superiority of spiritual gain. In this material world, the treasure of divine love has descended from Śrī Goloka Vṛndāvana (the spiritual realm) in the form of Śrī Harināma (the divine names of the Lord). If one engages in chanting these holy names of the Lord with love and devotion under the shelter of a genuine spiritual master, then gradually the desire for material comfort and enjoyment will be destroyed forever. One will develop an intense desire to serve Śrī Śrī Rādhā-Govinda, who are the supreme spiritual substance. Chanting the holy names of the Supreme Lord from the core of one's heart and engaging in the service of Śrī Śrī Rādhā-Govinda under the guidance and shelter of the *guru-paramparā* is considered to be the supreme spiritual benefit—*paramārtha*.

## 85
## What are the differences between *karma* (action/work), *jñāna* (knowledge), and *bhakti* (devotion)?

When we engage in any activity for the purpose of our own sense gratification, material profit, adoration, or status and position, then those actions are known as *karma*. In essence, *karma* is self motivated action, for it serves our own ends.

Knowledge is good, but it should not be of the nature of *advaita-jñāna*. In other words, it should not be used to achieve oneness with God or to merge with the Supreme Lord. True knowledge is to serve the Supreme Lord with love and devotion, which can never be realized if our aspiration is to become one with the Lord. Similarly, after acquiring knowledge, if one remains busy in serving his senses, then that knowledge is considered to be ignorance. We should never become a *jñāna-pāpī* (one who commits sin through the misuse of knowledge).

Devotion is superior to both *karma* and *jñāna*. Devotion is the original constitutional nature of the *jīvātmā*. Genuine devotion, when executed properly, takes us closer to the Supreme Lord and helps us experience eternal bliss, which we hanker after at every moment. This may be experienced when every action is performed for the pleasure of the Supreme Lord, Śrī Kṛṣṇa. Devotion, in summary, means to genuinely love the Supreme Lord and devote our entire being to His service.

Nowadays, by misinterpreting the true meaning of devotion, we are gradually cheating ourselves and distancing ourselves from the Supreme Lord.

We should clearly understand *karma* and *jñāna* as the antithesis of *bhakti*. That being said, when *karma* (action) and *jñāna* (knowledge) are perfectly subservient to *bhakti* (devotion), then their form is conducive for one's development in *bhakti*. And when they do not pollute *bhakti* by their ulterior motives, then this is still considered *śuddha-bhakti* (pure devotion). *Bhakti* (devotion) is actually considered the source of both *karma* and *jñāna* in their pure forms. Suppose someone gives me a *Bhagavad-gītā* or a *Śrīmad-Bhāgavatam*. If I didn't have any devotion, I wouldn't be inclined to read them. However, one who has a little devotion, in order to awaken more devotion, would immediately read those two books with full attention. This action of reading is considered to be *karma*. After reading with fixed attention, the knowledge that has been gained is considered to be *jñāna*. If I did not possess any devotion, then I would never have been inclined to read those books in the first place.

One who does not have knowledge is considered blind according to the revealed scriptures, so we should never think to give up knowledge completely. Let me give another example. If there is a diamond on the road, and if we don't have any specific knowledge in how to recognize diamonds, then we will totally neglect it, thinking it just a piece of glass. However, one equipped with knowledge will take advantage of their good fortune on finding such a valuable item.

I hope that this explanation has clearly described the differences between *karma, jñāna,* and *bhakti* for the readers.

## 86
## How do we know if we are progressing in our *bhajana* (devotional practice)?

Devotional practice means spiritual practice. According to our level of practice and our presiding state of consciousness, this will determine how much we are progressing. Ultimately, when we feel blissful in our spiritual practice, that is the symptom that we are progressing. In the beginning there may be so many *anarthas* (impediments), but gradually through the practice of devotion all such *anarthas* will dissipate and one's joy will increase.

## 87
## What is the significance of deity worship?

The main purpose of worship is to satisfy the deities. Deity worship means to serve the deity. Service means to satisfy the object of service. The significance of deity worship is to learn service following in the footsteps of our previous teachers. Our service is accepted by the deity via the medium of the previous teachers. Deity worship, in brief, means to learn the principle of *ānugatya* (subservience and obedience). In our current state in this material world, *ānugatya* means to serve the object of worship under the guidance of the previous teachers. Through the practice of *ānugatya* in the material world, we shall eventually attain service to the Supreme Lord in Goloka Vṛndāvana. There, in the spiritual world, we shall engage in the service of the Divine Couple, Śrī Śrī Rādhā-Kṛṣṇa, under the *ānugatya* of the intimate associates (*sakhīs*) of the Lord.

We must remember that if we do not chant the holy names, the deity will not accept any service from our hands. Consequently, deity worship engages us in chanting the holy names, which purifies our hearts and minds (*cittā*). By performing deity worship, we will eventually attain more taste for chanting the holy names. It also teaches us how to be clean internally and externally. Deity worship is meant to help us focus our minds on the spiritual abode, and gradually allows us to be free from material attachment.

## 88

## Offenses can wreak havoc in our spiritual life. How do we atone for offenses we make, even unwillingly?

As soon as we realize that we have committed an offense we have to feel deep regret. We must also rectify it to our best ability. For instance, if we realize later that we have committed an offense toward someone, we must beg that person for forgiveness. If that person is not physically present, then we must acknowledge his or her good qualities and glorify him or her. Such practice will allow us to atone for any offenses committed against another.

## 89
## What happens at the time of initiation between the guru and the disciple?

At the time of initiation, the disciple's mood should be of surrender to the *paramparā* through the initiating guru. This allows the initiating guru to give the disciple a connection to the *paramparā*. Such a connection will allow him to reach the abode of the Supreme Lord through the *paramparā's* mercy.

## 90
## If *harināma* is sufficient for deliverance from this material world, then what is the significance of the second initiation into the *gāyatrī-mantra*?

It is right to say that *kṛṣṇa-nāma* will allow us to attain Śrī Kṛṣṇa:

*kṛṣṇa-mantra haite habe saṁsāra-mocana*
*kṛṣṇa-nāma haite pābe kṛṣṇera caraṇa*

> By chanting the Hare Kṛṣṇa *mantra,* one can obtain freedom from material existence. Indeed, simply by chanting the holy name of Kṛṣṇa, one can attain the lotus feet of the Lord.
>
> *Śrī Caitanya-caritāmṛta* (*Ādi-līlā 7.73*)

*Harināma,* however, will only give full benefit when we are able to chant *śuddha-nāma* (the pure name). In other words, our chanting must be without any lingering traces of *anarthas,* meaning it is free from any material attachment and completely bereft of *aparādha* (offenses). Then we can get the fruit of chanting.

In essence, receiving the *gāyatrī-mantras* (second initiation) helps us to get rid of all the *anarthas,* which in turn helps us to chant the holy name purely. If we are chanting the *gāyatrī-mantras* with proper etiquette (sitting on an *āsana,* doing *ācamana,* etc.) as prescribed by the *guru-paramparā*, such *mantras* help to cure all our material attachments.

## 91

## Should *gṛhasthas* (householders) maintain the same standards of deity worship as those maintained in the temple?

The home is an *āśrama* and should be dedicated to the Lord. At home the householders have many responsibilities, such as maintaining a family and a job. If they can maintain their jobs and family life and it is manageable to keep the temple standard of worship, then it is all right to do so. They should first think about their family responsibilities, then they can set the standard of worship accordingly.

## 92
## How do we recognize a true *sādhu*?

A *śuddha-vaiṣṇava* (pure devotee) is a *sādhu*, but:

*vaiṣṇava chinite nāre debero śakati*

> Even gods and goddesses do not have the capacity to recognize a Vaiṣṇava.

We have to pray to the Lord to be able to recognize a genuine *sādhu*. The Lord will reveal this confidential truth in our hearts, and an inner intuition will confirm, "This is a true *sādhu*." If this positive intuition continues regarding this *sādhu*, then we can be sure that this is a true *sādhu*.

## 93
## Why are onion and garlic not consumed by devotees?

First of all, a devotee should only partake of food which is first offered to Kṛṣṇa. *Prasādam* (the Lord's remnants) can only be prepared from foods which are *sattvic* (in the mode of goodness) in nature. Onion and garlic are botanical members of the alliaceous (allium) family along with shallots, leeks, and chives. The traditional Vedic system of medicine, called Ayurveda, group all foods under one of the *tri-guṇas* (three primary material qualities): *sattva, rajas,* and *tamas*. Onion and garlic both fall in the *rajasic* and *tamasic* food groups, which are avoided by spiritual aspirants because they have adverse effects on the consciousness, which can be detrimental to devotion and spiritual progress.

It is a well-known fact that both onion and garlic are natural aphrodisiacs, which induce passion, aggression, agitation, and anxiety, making onion and garlic physically, emotionally, and spiritually harmful. For the spiritual aspirant, *sattva-guṇa* is recognized to be the best platform to practice *bhakti*. For this reason, Śrī Kṛṣṇa only accepts foods in *sattva-guṇa,* and as a result such food is elevated beyond the material quality of *sattva-guṇa* and becomes *prasādam,* the mercy of the Lord. Such *prasādam* should be consumed by spiritual aspirants.

The Purāṇas state how onion and garlic came

to be. Once, a *ṛṣi* named Balasava Ṛṣi, along with other *brāhmaṇas*, came together to perform a fire sacrifice. The use of the flesh and bones of an old cow was required to perform the sacrifice. In recompense for her self-sacrifice, the old cow was to be made young again by the power of the *brāhmaṇa's mantras*. During the fire sacrifice, Balasava Ṛṣi felt the call of nature, so he left to relieve himself.

While he was gone, his wife became overwhelmed with a desire to eat the flesh of the cow, and she requested a *brāhmaṇa* for a small piece thereof. Recognizing her impure desire and overwhelmed by guilt, she felt she could not return that portion, so she took the flesh and the bone and buried it in the ground. On completion of the sacrifice, Balasava Ṛṣi saw a young cow appear from the fire, but to his surprise, the cow's left side appeared smaller in size than the right. In order to know the reason, Balasava Ṛṣi sat in meditation and came to know of his wife's actions. On such a revelation, the Ṛṣi immediately ordered his wife to return what she had buried. Accompanying his wife, they both went to the burial place and saw that from the flesh appeared the onion family, from the bone appeared garlic, and from the blood appeared red lentils. From this time onward those three food items are considered to be non-vegetarian.

Even in Hindu temples dedicated to worshiping the Vedic gods and goddesses, one does not usually see offerings of onion, garlic, or red lentils as part of their worship. Vaiṣṇava devotees strictly do not offer such items to their Lordships, knowing that they will not be accepted.

## 94

## How can we show respect to everyone?

Respect means to honor the law and order set down by the supreme authority, and the supreme authority of all that exists is Śrī Kṛṣṇa. Śrī Kṛṣṇa, being the Supreme Lord, knows what is best for the welfare of all living beings, and He has created the four progressive stages of life called *āśramas*. It is the duty of all humans to follow the laws governed by these *āśramas*. These *āśramas* are the *brahmacārī-āśrama* (student life), the *gṛhastha-āśrama* (household life), the *vānaprastha-asrama* (retired life), and the *sannyāsa-āśrama* (the renounced order of life). Each of these *āśramas* has specific laws and duties associated with them, and we can see the integral interplay of respect in all of them. Let me give some examples.

In the duty of the *gṛhastha-āśrama*, the parents must look after the children, and when the parents become older, in return, it becomes the children's responsibility to look after their parents. As for a wife, the duty is to honor her husband as the master of the house; and as for the husband, he has to consider his wife to be the ornament of his family. Just as one would value and honor a beautiful ornament, the wife should be honored in a similar fashion by the husband.

In the *sannyāsa* order of life, one must observe the ways of spirituality and lead by example. *Sannyāsīs* should be engaged in the regulated chanting of the holy names, and be free from material desires, such as for name, fame, adoration, and so on. One should also practice humility and extreme tolerance and be the true well-wisher of all living beings, not only humans.

So in every aspect of life, respect is an integral part of how we deal with others and our environment—whether we are living in a temple, working at the office, or studying in school. Those living in the temple show respect by serving the deities, guru, and the Vaiṣṇavas with utmost focus. In the working world, whether we are employers or employees, respect should be given on the basis that we are all human beings and worthy of respect, regardless of age, abilities, race, status, and so on. Everyone should be engaged in specific and appropriate work. A good employer will exercise respect by thinking of the financial, physical, and personal well-being of the employee. In return, the employees will exhibit respect by their gratitude toward the fairness and generosity of the employer. As for teachers and students, the teacher should always think of how to best guide the students so that the students will excel in their education, and the students in turn should follow the curriculum set by the teacher.

We can see by this analysis that respect is the common thread for great success, peace, and harmony within society. I hope this helps the reader to understand the importance of respect in all facets of life.

## 95
## How can we respect those who have negative behaviors?

Due to Kali-yuga, the age of quarrel, most people have negative attributes. We possess limited intelligence as well as a limited duration of life—a maximum of one hundred years. We pass half our lives sleeping; we spend a decent portion in sickness; in childhood we are absorbed in childish activities; and in youth we are preoccupied with chasing the pleasures of youth. An intelligent person will understand that we do not have much time, and that we shouldn't waste it focusing on other people's negative behaviors. We should always remain optimistic. In order to maintain peace in society, we should show respect by maintaining extreme tolerance at all times and by trying our best to transform a person's negative behaviors into positive ones. As humans, we are expected to be true well-wishers of all living beings, so we should at least make three attempts at helping a person transform his or her behavior. If there are no positive results in our attempts, then we should keep our distance, and instead pray to the Lord for that person's upliftment.

## 96

## While performing *japa*, what should we meditate on? Is there a meditation for beginners? Is it different for intermediates and again different for devotees on the topmost platform?

According to our previous spiritual masters, whatever we think about while chanting will be our destination. Therefore we must meditate as per the information provided by the previous spiritual masters.

In the preliminary stage of chanting, we should hear the holy names and simultaneously think of the beautiful form of Śrī Śrī Rādhā-Kṛṣṇa. Eventually rising to the intermediary stage, one's mind will gravitate toward the attractive qualities of Śrī Śrī Rādhā-Kṛṣṇa and Their loving affection toward Their devotees. Then, as one progresses from the intermediate stage to the advanced stage, meditation on Śrī Śrī Radha-Kṛṣṇa's sweet pastimes (*līlā*) in Vṛndāvana will begin to manifest. The topmost stage is when we enter, in spirit, into the eternal pastimes of Śrī Śrī Rādhā-Kṛṣṇa. There we will render service in our *mañjarī-rūpa* (our eternal form) under the guidance of the *sakhīs*, headed by Lalitā Devī. At that time our eternal form will become manifest, along with our eternal age, outfit, and service. In this topmost stage, our physical form will remain in the material world, but in spirit we will be engaged in the eternal pastimes of the Divine Couple, Śrī Śrī Rādhā-Kṛṣṇa.

## 97
## What is free will?

When our will is free from the resistance of others or the interference of other forces, this is known as free will. In this world, only humans possess free will, and all other living beings (animals, birds, reptiles, etc.) are bound by instinct. For instance, creatures from the animal kingdom cannot choose their faith, nor do they possess the ability to question or understand whether there is a God or not. On the other hand, human beings are endowed with both the ability to understand and the free will to choose whether to be a theist or an atheist. They have the free will to believe in God as a Hindu, Muslim, Christian, Jew, and so on, or not to believe in God at all.

Association is the basis of what we gravitate toward in life. For example, if someone would like to become a doctor, then according to that person's free will, he will search out association of like-minded persons in the same field, and subsequently, becoming influenced by that association, will progress toward his goal. The same applies when choosing a spiritual path and adhering to that particular path. Sincere application to a spiritual path will be based purely on the free will of the individual.

## 98

## Why do we engage in *karma* (activity)?

First of all, we must understand the real meaning of *karma*. *Karma* means "activity." Energy is always moving and never stays in one place. So wherever energy is present, there must be action. Being present in the material world means that the material energy will always be pushing us toward material activities. When persons are influenced by material nature, they are engaged in the *karma* of this world.

Similarly, when persons are influenced by the spiritual nature, which is beyond the material nature, they are also engaged in a kind of *karma*, but for the satisfaction of God. This type of *karma* is categorized as *bhakti*. One type of *karma* is for our material gain and the other is for the pleasure of Kṛṣṇa. One way or another, we always have to act and be engaged in *karma*. This is inevitable. Either we are engaged in material *karma* or spiritual *karma*. The difference between the two *karmas* is that material *karma* bestows temporary results and spiritual *karma* awards eternal results.

## 99
## Why don't we get good association from the beginning?

As discussed earlier, we know that humans have free will. Not only that, but we possess the best of intelligence amid all earthly species. By that intelligence and freedom, we have the ability to choose with whom or what we associate, and the material world will present us with both good and bad association. As we can see in our present society, we have a choice of so many different faiths. Some will choose to chant Hare Kṛṣṇa, whereas others will choose to worship the goddess Kālī or Durgā, while many more will choose to follow Islam, Judaism, Christianity, and so on.

The strange thing is that all people, irrespective of their faith, feel that they are in good association. So we cannot say that we are not getting good association, for this depends on the level of one's faith and the influence of the association one keeps. To fully understand what good association is, we have to objectively examine and compare the various forms, as well as assess whether the information from our association is bona fide and authorized according to the ancient scriptures of the Vedas.

## 100
## Is there any way to destroy the consequences of bad *karma*?

Our destiny is determined by the consequences of our previous *karma*. For example, mango trees will grow only after mango seeds are planted. After cultivating the seeds with proper care, the seeds eventually grow into mango trees, which will only give mango fruits. Similarly, depending on our actions, whether favorable or unfavorable, we will reap the results accordingly. As it is said, you reap what you sow. Here are a few examples of how we reap the fruits of our actions. If one lives a life of hypocrisy, then the consequence of that behavior is that one may take birth as a snake in a deep forest. If one is shameless, the ramification of such action is that one may take on the form of a tree. And by being stubborn, one may be born as an elephant.

In this material world, the best *karma* is to please the Supreme Lord. According to scriptural information, the easiest way to please the Lord in this age of quarrel is by chanting His holy names—*vartamānaś ca yat pāpaṁ yat bhūtam yat bhaviṣyati tat sarvam nirdahatyāśu govindānala-kīrtanat* (*Hari-bhakti-vilāsa* 11.339, *Laghu Bhāgavata*). Whatever bad *karma* one has committed in the past, is committing in the present, and will commit in the future, along with all one's negative tendencies—all are absolutely destroyed by the chanting of the holy names of Govinda.

## 101
## Please explain the significance of our *japa-mālā*?

The *japa-mālā* represents Śrī Vṛndāvana-dhāma and particularly its most prominent residents. The beads represent Śrī Śrī Rādhā-Kṛṣṇa, the *sakhīs*, the *gopīs*, Paurṇamāsī, and Gopeśvara Śiva. This is verified as follows:

*sumeru yugalarūpam pārśve cāṣṭasakhīstatha*
*catuḥṣaṣṭigopikāñca dvātriṁśad gopabālakaḥ*
*vīravṛndā paurṇamāsī gopeśvara samanvitaṁ*
*evaṁ krameṇa malām hi satamaṣṭotaram japet*
*(Mantrārtha Cāndrikā)*

The *japa-mālā* has 108 beads. The bead on the very top is known as Sumeru, or the Sumeru bead, which represents Rādhā and Kṛṣṇa. The first eight beads are the eight principal *sakhīs*, Lalitā, Viśākhā, Citrā, Campakalatā, Raṅgadevī, Sudevī, Indulekhā, and Tuṅgavidyā. Each *sakhī* has eight assistants, making sixty-four assistants in total. Their names are given as follows:

(1) **Śrī Lalitā-sakhī's group**: Ratnaprabhā, Ratnakalā (Ratikalā), Subhadrā, Bhadrarekhikā (Candrarekhikā), Sumukhī, Dhaniṣṭhā, Kalahaṁsī, Kalāpinī

(2) **Śrī Viśākhā-sakhī's group**: Mādhavī, Mālatī, Candrarekhikā, Gurjarī (Kuñjarī), Hariṇī, Capalā, Surabhi, Śubhānanā

(3) **Śrī Sucitrā-sakhī's group**: Rasālikā, Tilakinī, Śaurasenī, Sugandhikā, Rāmilā (Kāmilā), Kāmanagarī, Nāgarī, Nāgabelikā

(4) **Śrī Indulekhā-sakhi's group**: Tuṅgabhadrā (Tuṅgavidyā), Rasatuṅgā, Raṅgabaṭī, Sumaṅgalā, Citralekhā, Vicitrāṅgī, Modanī, Madanālasā

(5) **Śrī Campakalatā-sakhī's group**: Kuraṅgākṣī, Sucaritā, Maṇḍalī, Maṇikuṇḍalā, Candrikā, Candratilakā (Candralatikā), Padmākṣī, Sumandirā

(6) **Śrī Raṅgadevī-sakhī's group**: Kalakaṇthī, Śaśikalā, Kamalā, Madhurī, Indurā, Kandarpa-sundarī, Kāmalatikā, Prema Mañjarī

(7) **Śrī Tuṅgavidyā-sakhī's group**: Mañjumedhā, Sumadhurā, Sumadhyā, Madhurekṣanā, Tanumadhyā, Madhutpannā, Guṇacūḍā, Varāṅgadā

(8) **Śrī Sudevī-sakhī's group**: Kāverī, Cārukavarī, Sukeśī, Mañjukeśikā, Hārahīrā, Mahāhīrā, Hārakaṇṭhī, Manoharā

The next thirty-two beads represent the prominent *gopa-bālakas*, Śrī Kṛṣṇa's friends. The last four beads represent Vīra Devī, Vṛndā Devī, Paurṇamāsī, and Gopeśvara Māhādeva.

The above description reveals the meaning of all 108 beads, and also shows how the *japa-mālā* represents Śrī Vṛndāvana-dhāma.

The theme of the beads is that there is a wish-fulfilling tree, under which there is a beautiful throne where Rādhā and Kṛṣṇa are sitting. They are surrounded by the eight principal *sakhīs*, who are serving Them with their assistants, as mentioned above.

## 102
## Can we meditate on any other form of the Lord, other than Kṛṣṇa, while chanting the *mahā-mantra*?

Apart from Kṛṣṇa, we may meditate on Caitanya Mahāprabhu and His associates while chanting. But apart from Caitanya Mahāprabhu and His associates, it is better not to think about other forms of the Lord, because the holy name has the power of a wish-fulfilling stone. Whatever we think about during chanting will be our destination. So if we think about other personalities rather than Rādhā and Kṛṣṇa while chanting, then we will not achieve the highest abode of Goloka Vṛndāvana.

## 103
## Some advocate that by chanting sixteen rounds one can attain the lotus feet of Śrī Kṛṣṇa. Others emphasize sixty-four rounds. What are your thoughts?

The most important point is to chant with purity. Our goal is not to reach numbers; our goal is to reach Goloka Vṛndāvana. The divine wealth of Goloka Vṛndāvana—*golokera premadhana*—is the Hare Kṛṣṇa *mahā-mantra*. We know from *Śrī Caitanya Bhāgavata* that Lord Caitanya manifested a pastime in which He instructed His associates to chant sixty-four rounds every day, known as *lakh-nāma*. As we are followers of Caitanya Mahāprabhu, it is optimal for us to chant a minimum of sixty-four rounds attentively every day. I hope the readers will understand the points mentioned herein.

## 104
## Is it possible to attain *kṛṣṇa-prema* through the other limbs of *bhakti* while neglecting the chanting of the *mahā-mantra*?

I have repeatedly heard from my spiritual master, His Divine Grace Śrīla Bhakti Pramode Purī Gosvāmī Ṭhākura, and from my grand spiritual master, His Divine Grace Śrīla Prabhupāda Bhaktisiddhānta Sarasvatī Gosvāmī Ṭhākura, about the primary importance of chanting the holy names, as described in *Śrī-Caitanya-caritāmṛta* (*Madhya-līlā* 22.128–29):

*sādhu-saṅga, nāma-kīrtana, bhāgavata-śravaṇa*
*mathurā-vāsa, śrī-mūrtira śraddhāya sevana*
*sakala-sādhana-śreṣṭha ei pañca aṅga*
*kṛṣṇa-prema janmāya ei pāñcera alpa saṅga*

These five limbs of devotion, namely associating with seekers of the absolute truth,

> chanting the holy names, listening to *Śrīmad-Bhāgavatam*, residing in Mathurā-maṇḍala and worshiping the deity of the Lord with faith are the best among all spiritual practices. Just a bit of association with these five limbs of devotion give rise to pure love for Śrī Kṛṣṇa.

Again, we see the following in *Śrī Caitanya-caritāmṛta* (*Antya-līlā* 4.70–71):

> *bhajanera madhye śreṣṭha nava-vidhā bhakti*
> *'kṛṣṇa-prema', 'kṛṣṇa' dite dhare mahā-śakti*
> *tāra madhye sarva-śreṣṭha nāma-saṅkīrtana*
> *niraparādhe nāma laile pāya prema-dhana*

> Among all practices of devotion, the nine limbs of devotion are considered the best. They have immense power to give Kṛṣṇa to the worshiper and to bestow pure love for Kṛṣṇa on him. Among these nine limbs of devotion, the best is chanting the holy names. If one chants the holy names free of offenses, then he attains the treasure of pure love for Kṛṣṇa.

His Divine Grace Śrīla Prabhupāda Bhaktisiddhānta Sarasvatī Gosvāmī Ṭhākura has stated the following in his instructions: "None of the five limbs of devotion mentioned above, such as living in Mathurā-maṇḍala, associating with *sādhus*, etc., are complete without the chanting of the holy names of Śrī Kṛṣṇa. However, if we engage solely in chanting the holy names of Kṛṣṇa, then we can attain all the fruits that are born of residing in Mathurā-maṇḍala, associating with devotees, worshiping the deity with faith, and listening to the *Śrīmad-Bhāgavatam*. Worshiping the Supreme Lord through chanting His holy names is the highest perfection for all living entities."

We cannot say that *saṅkīrtana* is the only way, but it is surely the easiest way to achieve *prema* in this age of Kali.

## 105
## Can we achieve love for God without *sādhana*?

It is practically impossible. However, if we get immense mercy (*kṛpa*) from a highly elevated Vaiṣṇava, then we may get love for God.

## 106
## What are Vaiṣṇava qualities and how do they appear in the aspirant's heart?

In brief, Lord Kṛṣṇa in the form of Caitanya Mahāprabhu has stated in His *Śikṣāṣṭakam*, verse 3:

*tṛṇād api su-nīcena*
*taror iva sahiṣṇunā*
*amāninā mānadena*
*kīrtanīyaḥ sadā hariḥ*

One should be humbler than a blade of grass and more tolerant than a tree. One should be free of all material desire, such as desiring name, fame, position, worship, etc. One should offer due respect to everyone. In this way, one should constantly chant the Hare Kṛṣṇa *mahā-mantra*.

Also, we have seen in the *Śrī-Caitanya-caritāmṛta* (*Madhya-līlā* 22.78–80) that there are twenty-six Vaiṣṇava qualities:

*kṛpālu, akṛta-droha, satya-sāra, sama*
*nidoṣa, vadānya, mṛdu, śuci, akiñcana*
*sarvopakāraka, śānta, kṛṣṇaika-śaraṇa*
*akāma, anīha, sthira, vijita-ṣaḍ-guṇa*
*mita-bhuk, apramatta, mānada, amānī*
*gambhīra, karuṇa, maitra, kavi, dakṣa, maunī*

The twenty-six Vaiṣṇava qualities are as follows: being merciful, free of enmity, completely truthful, equal, faultless, magnanimous, soft in every aspect, clean, having no material possessions, being helpful to all, peaceful, having Kṛṣṇa as the one and only shelter, being free of lust, being indifferent to material possessions, being fixed, having conquered the six negative qualities (lust, anger, greed, bewilderment, madness, and envy), eating only as much as is required, being free of pride, offering respect to all, not expecting respect, being grave, sympathetic, friendly, poetic, expert, and silent.

Among those twenty-six qualities, there is the quality of *kṛṣṇaika-śaraṇa* which means to take exclusive shelter of Śrī Kṛṣṇa. By *kṛṣṇaika-śaraṇa,* along with constantly chanting the Hare Kṛṣṇa *mahā-mantra,* we will then spontaneously develop these Vaiṣṇava qualities.

## 107

## Sometimes we meet people in the community of devotees claiming to have much affection for the Lord, but with further examination, we see that their behavior conflicts with such claims. How do we recognize genuine devotion?

Devotion is like a diamond, and a diamond is very precious. If we possess a diamond, then it is natural that we will keep the diamond hidden and in a safe place. We will not exhibit the diamond to the whole world in fear of it getting stolen. In the same manner, those who have genuine devotion will never publicly declare their affection for the Lord. Instead, they will secretly keep such devotion within their hearts, thinking devotion even more precious than a diamond. Mahāprabhu, even though He is the Supreme Lord, never claimed to have exalted feelings of devotion. Instead, He taught us how to recognize pure devotion in His *Śikṣāṣṭakam*, verse 6.

*nayanaṁ galad-aśru-dhārayā*
*vadanaṁ gadgada-ruddhayā girā*
*pulakair nicitaṁ vapuḥ kadā*
*tava nāma-grahaṇe bhaviṣyati*

> When will tears flow from My eyes? When will My voice choke up? When will My hairs stand on end on chanting Your holy names?

There is no pretense in pure devotion. Real devotion will bestow on us blissful realizations and the ability to relish devotional practice. When one has pure devotion, one's devotional feelings can never change and one is always absorbed in the service of the Lord.

Humility, tolerance, being free from the desire for material recognition, such as name, fame, and adoration, respecting everyone without discrimination, and constantly chanting the *mahā-mantra*—these are the qualities of pure devotion that we should be observing in our hearts. We should not make a show of great devotion for the sake of our own self-aggrandizement. If we do, then even if we once had a genuine glimpse of realization of the Supreme, we will lose it. Contrary to genuine devotion, the results of pretense only bring embarrassment in the long run.

## 108

## Kṛṣṇa explains in the *Bhagavad-gītā*, "One who remembers Me at the time of death will come to Me." What type of consciousness does a person have to be in for this claim of Kṛṣṇa's to come true? Can anyone achieve this, even if he or she did not cultivate devotion?

Lord Kṛṣṇa says in the *Bhagavad-gītā* (8.6):

*yaṁ yaṁ vāpi smaran bhāvaṁ*
*tyajaty ante kalevaram*
*taṁ tam evaiti kaunteya*
*sadā tad-bhāva-bhāvitaḥ*

One's consciousness at the time of death determines one's next destination. One must be conscious of Kṛṣṇa at the time of death to remember Him. But we should keep in mind that without the perfection of spiritual practice (*sādhana-siddhi*) no one can reach the abode of the Supreme Lord. As we have seen in the story of Ajāmila, even though he chanted the holy name of Nārāyaṇa at the time of death, still he was not qualified to enter the abode of the Supreme Lord. The messengers of Lord Viṣṇu kept him in Haridvāra for twelve years, where he engaged in spiritual practice.

# SANSKRIT PRONUNCIATION

The short vowel ***a*** is pronounced like the ***u*** in b***u***t, the long ā like the ***a*** in f***a***r.

The short ***i*** is pronounced as in p***i***n, the long ***ī*** as in p***i***que, the short ***u*** as in p***u***ll, and the long ***ū*** as in r***u***le.

The vowel ***ṛ*** is pronounced like the **ri** in **ri**m, the ***e*** like the ***ey*** in *th**ey***, the ***o*** like the ***o*** in g***o***, the ***ai*** like the ***ai*** in ***ai***sle, and the ***au*** like the ***ow*** in h***ow***.

The *anusvara* (***ṁ***) is pronounced like the ***n*** in the French word ***bon,*** and the *visarga* (***ḥ***) is pronounced as a final ***h*** sound. At the end of a couplet, ***aḥ*** is pronounced ***aha***, and ***iḥ*** as ***ihi.***

The guttural consonants—***k***, ***kh***, ***g***, ***gh,*** and ***ṅ***—are pronounced from the throat in much the same manner as in English. ***K*** is pronounced as in ***k***ite, ***kh*** as in Ec***kh***art, ***g*** as in ***g***ive, ***gh*** as in di***g-h***art, ***ṅ*** as in si***ng***.

The palatal consonants—***c, ch, j, jh,*** and ñ—are pronounced with the tongue touching the firm ridge behind the teeth. ***C*** is pronounced as in ***ch***air, ***ch*** as in staun***ch-h***eart, ***j*** as in ***j***oy, ***jh*** as in hed**geh**og, and ñ as in ca***ny***on.

The cerebral consonants—***ṭ, ṭh, ḍ, ḍh,*** and ***ṇ***—are pronounced with the tip of the tongue turned up and drawn back against the dome of the palate. ***Ṭ*** is pronounced as in **t**ub, ***ṭh*** as in ligh***t-h***eart, ***ḍ*** as in ***d***ove, ***ḍh*** as in re***d-h***ot, and ***ṇ*** as in ***n***ut.

The dental consonants—***t, th, d, dh,*** and ***n***—are pronounced in the same manner as the cerebrals but with the forepart of the tongue against the teeth.

The labial consonants—***p, ph, b, bh,*** and ***m***—are pronounced with the lips. ***P*** is pronounced as in ***p***ine, ***ph*** as in u***ph***ill, ***b*** as in ***b***ird, ***bh*** as in ru***b-h***ard, and ***m*** as in ***m***other.

The semi-vowels—***y, r, l,*** and ***v***—are pronounced as in ***y***es, ***r***un, ***l***ight, and ***v***ine, while the sibilants—ś, ***ṣ,*** and ***s***—are pronounced as in the German ***s***prechen, ***sh***ine, and ***s***un. ***H*** is as in ***h***ome.

# Short Biographies of Our Lineage

## Lord Śrī Caitanya Mahāprabhu

In 1486, the Supreme Lord Śrī Kṛṣṇa manifested the pastime of taking birth in Māyāpur Nadia, West Bengal, in the form of Lord Caitanya. Around the time of His birth, the social system of India was in turbulence. All the rulers were unnecessarily torturing the citizens, and the *brāhmaṇas* were misusing their position and mistreating others from other castes. During that period, Lord Caitanya appeared with the purpose of enlightening the world—to help people understand that we are all living entities coming from the Lord's existence in the form of the soul, like tiny fire sparks. Therefore He wanted us to look beyond race, color, creed, and caste, and stop all types of discrimination against one another, especially giving up all the hate that we may hold for one another. He wanted us to understand that we should respect and see everyone as eternal servants of the Lord, and that the goal of life is to always fix our minds in the service of the Lord. He also taught that we should maintain our material duties with our parents, children, husband, wife, neighbors, and relatives without attachment. Alongside our material duties we should practice spirituality instead of fighting one another in the name of religion and false prestige. In order to practice spirituality in this Age of Kali, and to bring peace and harmony to society, He instructed us to chant the Hare Kṛṣṇa *mahā-mantra:*

*Hare Kṛṣṇa Hare Kṛṣṇa Kṛṣṇa Kṛṣṇa Hare Hare*
*Hare Rāma Hare Rāma Rāma Rāma Hare Hare*

He remained physically present on earth from 1486 to 1534. For the first twenty-four years, He performed His childhood pastimes and as a young man He lived as a householder. For the last twenty-four years of His manifest pastimes, He was in the renounced order (*sannyāsa*).

In 1534, He went back to His spiritual abode through the pastime of disappearing from this world simultaneously from three different locations. He merged into the body of the Lord Jagannātha deity in Jagannātha Purī; He entered into the deity of Toṭa Gopīnātha; and He disappeared from the vision of observers while walking into the Mahodadhi Ocean. These three occurrences miraculously took place in Jagannātha Purī. Just as the Lord enters this world by His own sweet will, in the same way He can also mysteriously disappear from this world.

## Śrīla Bhaktivinoda Ṭhākura

Śrīla Bhaktivinoda Ṭhākura was born as Kedarnātha Datta on the 2nd of September 1838, and belonged to a wealthy *jamindar* (landlord) family. In his early years he was exceptionally studious. In his university days he associated with the intellectuals of the Bengali Renaissance. He studied numerous philosophical systems of both the East and the West, and was also an accomplished poet. His career culminated in his post as District Magistrate, which was the highest post available to a native Indian under the rule of the British Raja. In his 29th year, he became a dedicated follower of Śrī Caitanya

Mahāprabhu, and very quickly established himself as a prominent and influential member of the Gauḍīya Vaiṣṇava community. Always thinking of how to present Mahāprabhu's teachings to a modern world, he authored over one hundred books. He laid the foundation for Gauḍīya Vaiṣṇavism's eventual global dissemination. He departed this world on the 23rd of June 1914, leaving his legacy in the hands of his son Śrīla Prabhupāda Bhaktisiddhānta Sarasvatī Ṭhākura.

## Śrīla Bhaktisiddhānta Sarasvatī Ṭhākura

Śrīla Prabhupāda was born as Bimala Prasāda Datta, on Friday, the 6th of February 1874, in the vicinity of Lord Jagannātha's temple, in Orissa. From his childhood, he practiced devotion under the guidance of his parents: his father, Śrī Kedarnātha Datta (famously known as Śrīla Bhaktivinoda Ṭhākura) and mother, Bhāgavatī Devī. Bimala Prasāda took a vow to chant one billion holy names of the Hare Kṛṣṇa *mahā-mantra* before undertaking the task of spreading the loving message of Lord

Caitanya. In 1918, he took the renounced order (*sannyāsa*) and became Śrīla Bhaktisiddhānta Sarasvatī. At that time he established his first preaching center, Śrī Caitanya Maṭha, in Māyāpur. In 1918, the scholarly Vaiṣṇava community gave him the devotional title Śrīla Prabhupāda. In a short period, many intellectual stalwarts joined his fledgling movement, many of whom also entered the renounced order to assist him in spreading the loving mission of Lord Caitanya. He eventually established sixty-four centers in India and abroad in the name of Śrī Gauḍīya Maṭha. Śrīla Prabhupāda, the life and soul of the Gauḍīya Maṭha, physically passed away at the Bagh Bazaar, Kolkata, Gauḍīya Maṭha on January 1, 1937 at 5.30 A.M.

## Śrīla Bhakti Pramode Purī Gosvāmī Ṭhākura

My spiritual master was born as Pramode Bhushan Chakrabarty on Wednesday, the 18th of October 1898, at Ganganandapur village, Jessor district, in present day Bangladesh. In his childhood Pramode Bhushan was inspired to practice devotion by his neighbor, Bhakti Ratna Ṭhākura, the godbrother of Śrīla Bhaktivinoda Ṭhākura. In 1915, he met with Bimala Prasāda. In 1919, he completed a bachelor's degree in science at Kolkata University. In 1921, he joined Śrīla Prabhupāda's mission, and in 1923 he was formally initiated. He received the name Praṇavānanda Dāsa Brahmacārī, and assumed service in the publications department. In 1947, he received the renounced order from his godbrother, Śrīla Bhakti Gaurav Vaikhānasa Mahārāja, and received the name Bhakti Pramode Purī. In 1958, the ancient temple named Śrī Ananta Vāsudeva in Kālnā, Nadia, West Bengal was donated to him. From 1961 to 1994, he stayed with Śrīla Bhakti Dayitā Mādhava Gosvāmī Mahārāja, the founder of Śrī Caitanya Gauḍīya Maṭha. Eventually, in 1987, he established Śrī Gopīnātha Gauḍīya Maṭha in Māyāpur, Nadia. Unfortunately, while staying at Gopīnātha Gauḍīya Maṭha's Jagannātha Purī branch, at 2:10 A.M. on Friday the 22nd of November 1999, he physically departed from this world.

# About the Author

His Holiness Śrīla Bhakti Bibudha Bodhāyan Gosvāmī Mahārāja is the current President Ācārya of Śrī Gopīnātha Gauḍīya Maṭha. He is the successor of the great saint Śrīla Bhakti Pramode Purī Gosvāmī Ṭhākura.

He was born Asim Kumar Sau on August 21, 1964, in Kanpur, West Bengal, India. Born into a Vaiṣṇava family, from his earliest years he practiced *bhakti* under the guidance of his maternal grandfather, Śrīmān Madana Mohana Prabhu who was a stalwart disciple of Śrīla Prabhupāda Bhaktisiddhānta Sarasvatī Ṭhākura. Although his paternal family all worshiped Śakti in the form of Kālī, Asim was heavily influenced by the devotion of his grandfather. In this way, he was inclined to the worship of Śrī Śrī Rādhā-Kṛṣṇa in the mood of Śrī Caitanya Mahāprabhu, following in the line of Śrīla Prabhupāda.

In 1978, while Asim was at the tender age of fourteen, Śrīmān Madana Mohana Prabhu took a contingent of over forty family members to Śrī Dhāma Māyāpur to celebrate the appearance festival of Śrīmān Mahāprabhu. While visiting the Yoga-pīṭha, birthplace of Śrī Caitanya, on the Lord's appearance day, and seeing so many learned devotees and *sannyāsīs* and hearing their divine discourses, Asim vowed to dedicate his life to the path of devotion. He envisioned himself one day entering the *sannyāsa-āśrama*. Unsure how his family would react to such an idea, he kept it a secret.

By this time Asim had already met the illustrious devotee, Śrīla Bhakti Pramode Purī Gosvāmī Ṭhākura, and in his heart, had accepted him as his *dīkṣā-guru*. Shortly after his epiphany at the Yoga-pīṭha, Asim thought, "Let me quit worldly life and surrender unto the lotus feet of Śrī Guru." In this way, one day he stayed away from school with a desire to meet Śrīla B. P. Purī Gosvāmī Ṭhākura. On arriving there, the Ṭhākura was engaged in his daily worship. Asim waited and watched him in awe for several hours not wanting to disrupt his meditation. Once he had finished his worship, he gave Asim full attention.

When Asim revealed his mind, the Ṭhākura replied, "You are an intelligent boy. You should complete your education before making such an important life decision." Acknowledging the good sense of such guidance, Asim again resolved himself to follow the order of his guru and complete his education. He went on to complete a Bachelor of Commerce at Kolkata University.

All the while, his devotion never waned. In January 1986, he received *nāma* initiation from Śrīla B. P. Purī Gosvāmī Ṭhākura. He was given the name Acyutānanda Dāsa. In January 1990, during the auspicious festivities of the appearance festival of Śrī Caitanya Mahaprabhu, he received initiation into the *gāyatrī-mantra.*

Śrīla B. P. Purī Gosvāmī Ṭhākura was gradually attracting a considerable following. The devotees, headed by Acyutānanda's family, repeatedly requested him to open a temple so that they could have a place to gather. After many requests, he relented by strictly stipulating that such an establishment should only be for *bhajana*—deep spiritual practice.

In May 1990, Śrī Gopīnātha Gauḍīya Maṭha held its grand opening and the deities of Śrī Śrī Rādhā-Gopīnātha, Śrī Jagannātha-Baladeva-Subhadrā, and Lakṣmī-Narasiṁhadeva were installed. During the festivities, Acyutānanda and his father met with Śrīla B. P. Purī Gosvāmī Ṭhākura. He said to Acyutānanda's father, "Baba Sunil Kṛṣṇa, may I ask you a question?" He replied, "Yes, Gurudeva." The Ṭhākura continued, "You have four sons. Would you have any objection if I kept Asim with me for my personal services?" His father replied, "It would bring us much happiness if Asim decided to stay and engage in such perfect *sevā* (service) for you." On the 28th of May 1990, Acyutānanda left home and became the personal servant of his guru.

Acyutānanda was primarily engaged in direct service to his guru, but he also engaged in managing the affairs of the *maṭha*. In 1993, at the insistence of his guru, he accepted the renounced order of *sannyāsa* and received the name Tridaṇḍī Bhikṣu Bhakti Bibudha Bodhāyan. He then started traveling and preaching extensively, making his first sojourns to foreign lands.

On Gaura Pūrṇimā, in the year 1997, Śrīla Bhakti Pramode Purī Gosvāmī Ṭhākura announced that Śrīla Bhakti Bibudha Bodhāyan would become his successor. On October 22, 1999, Śrīla B. P. Purī Gosvāmī Ṭhākura left this world to reenter the spiritual realm. From this time onwards, Śrīla B. B. Bodhāyan Mahārāja has been guiding Śrī Gopīnātha Gauḍīya

Maṭha as well as his disciples and followers through his perfect example and divine teachings. He travels the world tirelessly in order to spread Śrīmān Mahāprabhu's message of divine love for Śrī Śrī Rādhā-Kṛṣṇa.